CRAZY

— OR —

GENIUS?

MARTIN KARAFILIS

CRAZY

— OR —

GENIUS?

NAVIGATING THE THIN LINE BETWEEN
BRILLIANCE AND MADNESS

First published in 2025 by Dean Publishing
PO Box 119
Mt. Macedon, Victoria, 3441
Australia
deanpublishing.com

DEAN PUBLISHING

Cataloguing-in-Publication Data
National Library of Australia
Title: Crazy or Genius?
Edition: 1st edn
ISBN: 978-1-925452-93-8
Category: Business/entrepreneurship

DEDICATION

To my son, Charlie Karafilis.

Throughout this journey, each challenge I've faced and every success I've celebrated has been driven by my hope to create a better future. One that I hope you can be proud of. You are my greatest motivation and my deepest joy. If, through my efforts, you can one day look up and say, "He's the best dad anyone could ever have," then I will have succeeded far beyond any business triumph.

This book is for you, Charlie. May it one day help guide you, inspire you, and show you how much you mean to me.

Your dad.

CONTENTS

NOT YOUR TYPICAL BUSINESS BOOK

A re you an entrepreneur or business owner who wants to know the key philosophies that can propel you to the highest tiers of success? Perhaps you're just starting out on your entrepreneurial journey and want to make sure you're fully equipped for the tough road ahead. Or maybe you've already achieved some success and want to ensure your winning streak continues. Wherever you are on your journey, you can breathe a sigh of relief because you've picked up my book – that is, the *right* book – which is the first step to getting you to the next level. The next step, as you might have guessed, is to *read it* and absorb and integrate the philosophies within. Simple, right?

Crazy or Genius? isn't a book about all the technical aspects of building and scaling a startup. There are plenty of other resources out there that will give you that information. Instead, I've chosen to share the key philosophies that have propelled me from a broke would-be entrepreneur, who quit his day job to risk it all on a crazy idea, to a serial success story. Why? Because every industry is different. Every business is different. Every person is different. The steps I took to set up and scale my business may not be relevant to yours.

So, instead of giving you a highly detailed business blueprint that may or may not apply to you and your unique situation, I'm sharing my winning philosophies, which anyone can apply to any business and, essentially, any life. Let's face it – when you're neck-deep in a project you're passionate about, it becomes your life. So, the beliefs by which I run my businesses also help me navigate my personal life, as they will help you at every step of your entrepreneurial journey, both personally and professionally.

Through trial, error, more error, and finally success, I've gained insights that will make the rough roads of entrepreneurship a whole lot smoother for you. Naturally, you'll still have to do the legwork but if you're ever struggling, if you're ever in doubt, if you're ever ready to throw in the towel, the advice in this book will help you keep pushing forward to reach that next level. I've dragged myself from the lonely bottom to the dizzying top of the entrepreneurial ladder, and I'm intimately familiar with every rung along the way. I know what works, and what doesn't. Importantly, I understand the underlying beliefs you need to cultivate to hit the pinnacle of success – and stay there. The staying there part is important.

It might shock you to learn that my philosophies didn't form overnight. Crazy, right? Man, if only I had known then what I know now, I could have saved myself a lot of, let's say, educational moments. Essentially, I've learnt the hard way so you don't have to.

All right, I'm not going to drag this introduction out any longer when we've got so much to discuss. By the end of this book, you'll have the core philosophies you need to be an unstoppable force in the business world. You'll be fully equipped to ascend to the top tiers of success. Quite frankly, your industry won't know what hit it.

Let the journey begin!

PHILOSOPHY

1

YOU'RE EITHER CRAZY, OR YOU'RE A GENIUS

CRAZY, GENIUS, OR JUST PLAIN STUPID?

Whenever we try to do something truly entrepreneurial, we either end up looking like a crazy person or a genius. Okay, I'll admit, sometimes we just look plain stupid. I'm sure most of us have earned that label a few times, yeah? So, what determines the label we ultimately receive? *The outcome*. It's all about the outcome. You could come up with the most insane idea anyone's ever heard and if you manage to pull it off, you're an instant genius. If, however, you fail to make the concept work, you're just another crazy person with a wacky idea that never went anywhere.

Fail, and people will say, "I always knew that guy was crazy!" But succeed, and you'll have the exact same people saying, "I always knew he was a genius!" Different outcomes earn different labels.

In business, the line between craziness and genius can get a little blurry. Some genius ideas seem crazy. Some crazy ideas seem genius. Sometimes, waiting for the outcome to determine which category your idea falls into isn't practical. For example, if you've gone all-in on an insane idea that's never going to work, you've likely just wasted a lot of time and money. And if you're holding back on a genuinely genius idea, you might miss the opportunity to put something amazing out into the world. That's why determining where your idea stands as soon as possible is so important. Don't worry, I've got a few tips to share on that one.

To be a successful entrepreneur, you've got to be a little crazy. You can't push boundaries and create a genuine impact if you don't have at least a tiny streak of madness in you. The key is knowing how to sort the utterly insane ideas from those that are bloody brilliant. It's a skill that all entrepreneurs should learn as early as possible. So, in this chapter, I'll share some of my greatest successes and biggest failures, and explain how you can determine whether an idea has legs before you take it too far.

THE DINNER PARTY OF DOUBT

When I first quit my job to focus on Tiliter (my first highly successful business) full-time, I had a difficult time convincing people I wasn't crazy. The business was still in the startup phase, and it was far from a guaranteed success. Still, I was certain we were onto something, so making the commitment was easy for me. However, explaining myself to others was much more difficult.

I remember being at a dinner party with a bunch of people who were friends but not close friends. We didn't know the intimate details of one another's lives. They were all well-paid professionals – lawyers, accountants, executives – working in the corporate world. At one point during the night, they were all discussing their careers and what they were working on. Eventually, it was my turn to talk. How did I even begin to explain that I had quit my job to focus on a startup company? I tried as best I could, hoping someone would understand. Silence. No one knew what to say. Suddenly, I felt very out of place. These were a bunch of highly successful people, all climbing the corporate ladder to even greater success, and here I was going all-in on an unknown startup. That night, I must have seemed like the craziest person in the room.

Once the initial shock wore off, a few people wished me luck, while others tried to talk me out of it. Most were visibly unimpressed. They couldn't understand someone not wanting to play the corporate game and become the top whatever in a big company. To them, I was throwing my life away. When you first embark on your entrepreneurial journey, you're going to get a lot of doubt from people. I'm here to tell you now, it's a part of the package. You may even doubt yourself at times. But if you've got that winning idea and you start to bring it to life, attitudes will begin to shift.

When we, as a business, started appearing in the media, gaining customer traction, and getting our product out there, we noticed the doubt drying up. Suddenly, our detractors were some of our biggest supporters. Who'd have thought? Once we started winning over the doubters, we knew we were on the right path. I went from being an absolute idiot – in their eyes! – to having an awesome idea that totally made sense. The attitude shift was unreal.

If I had let the doubt get to me at the start, Tiliter never would have succeeded, and I never would have found out if my idea was as insane as people thought or if I was onto a winner. Thankfully, I stuck to my guns and eventually breathed a sigh of relief when I didn't have to wear the crazy label.

During that awkward dinner party, I didn't know what the outcome of my big gamble would be. I did, however, have an inkling that I wasn't completely insane. That's why sticking to your guns is so important when you have an idea you believe in. In the beginning, it doesn't matter what others think. You don't need to win everyone over right away.

NEXT ROUND OF DOUBT

Don't think the doubt stops once you've converted those initial critics. It doesn't. Eventually, you'll need to start convincing investors that your idea isn't insane. Most of them will actually think you're crazy. Or stupid. Even if your idea is solid, you'll likely need to pitch to hundreds of investors before you find one who's willing to take a risk on you and your product.

You'll hear a lot of different reasons why they can't invest. Too ambitious. Too hard. Too uncertain. But don't let that put you off. It's normal to get *a lot* of noes before you get that golden yes. We knew we'd reached another turning point when investors who had originally said no came back a year or so later and asked to get in on the next round of investing. So, that was another group converted – but the doubt didn't end there.

Finally, you'll need to win over potential customers. All of that personal and financial support won't amount to much if no one wants to purchase your product, right? In our case, we had potential customers telling us how underdeveloped our technology was. They weren't wrong, but they failed to look to the future and understand where we were headed. The executives at one big corporation practically laughed us out of the room. Two years later, they became our biggest customer. At that point, we had pretty much cemented our idea as not crazy, perhaps even genius, and won over everyone who mattered.

What's the lesson here? Don't immediately rely on external forces to determine the validity of your idea. Give it time. You're going to meet doubt every step of the way. It all comes down to execution. Executing an idea is the riskiest part of running a business, but it's also how you reach an outcome. If you care about an idea enough to follow through and you really fight to make it happen, proving the doubters wrong, congratulations! You've crossed the line between crazy and genius and, importantly, ended up on the winning side.

DEALING WITH DOUBTERS

Early on, I think spite tends to fuel a lot of entrepreneurs. We want to prove the doubters wrong. We want to show that we're not crazy. Ultimately, we want to win. When we genuinely believe in an idea, all the doubt in the world can't hold us back. The doubters and the detractors, they're just fuel for the fire.

Harnessing the hate can be useful in the beginning, but you should be cautious about letting the trend continue. Eventually, a time will come when you need to stop worrying about what others are saying and focus purely on what you're doing. Yes, spite can be a powerful motivator but if you rely on it for too long, you risk hurting yourself and your business. Don't let it be the only fuel pushing you forward.

To be a really successful entrepreneur, you have to want to win. That desire to succeed at all costs will drive you when things get tough, doubt starts to creep in, and you start to think you might be crazy after all. I've been playing sports for most of my life, and the mentality is similar. The world's best athletes train for ten hours a day. Their diets are absolutely perfect. They're living and breathing their sport of choice. All of their focus is directed towards being the best they can be so they can *win*. The people in business who create the most impact adopt the same mindset. They want to win at all costs, and they'll give anything for success.

Many people will talk themselves out of a genius idea, convincing themselves it's crazy. They can't handle the doubt, the resistance, the effort, the risk – the list goes on. However, the most successful entrepreneurs know when to double down, push through the noise, and take their idea to the next level.

MY TRAIL OF FAILED STARTUPS

On the road to creating Tiliter, I left a trail of failed startups in my wake. That's right. My first idea wasn't a success. Nor was the one after that. I had to fail quickly at several businesses before I found one that got traction. Were my ideas too crazy? I don't think so. If anything, they weren't crazy enough. I didn't feel like I was creating something truly exciting, so I struggled to see the ideas through. In the end, the passion just wasn't there.

If you have an entrepreneurial mind, settling for anything short of exceptional is going to be difficult. You want to create change. You want to make an impact. You want to break down barriers and step outside of the norm. If you have an entrepreneurial mind, you're not going to be satisfied performing mundane tasks at a regular job. You're not even going to be satisfied owning and running a business – even one that's highly successful – if it isn't challenging you and breaking new ground. Honestly, to be a disruptive entrepreneur, you have to be just crazy enough to think you can change the world but sane enough to nail the execution on whatever world-changing idea you choose to pursue. Yep, it's a fine line.

Audio Hire Company

Really, my first business was the band I started when I was 16 years old. We were an acoustic duo, and the second guitarist was none other than Tiliter co-founder Chris. We'll talk more about the band itself a bit later. It was a pivotal part of my life, and I learnt a lot about business, marketing, and making the magic happen at all costs.

What I want to discuss now is the side hustle that came about during those band days: an innovative audio hire company. You might be asking, *What could possibly be innovative about an audio hire company?* Well, a lot of musicians had gear they weren't always using, which meant a lot of equipment was just sitting around, going to waste. So, I created a marketplace where people could rent out their spare equipment to other musicians. For bands that didn't have the money to buy all their gear outright or didn't have the space to store it, the platform was quite useful.

I started by putting my own gear up for rent, and people actually began using the service. As more people jumped on board, I realised that scaling would take a lot of capital and a lot of my time. Was I passionate enough to make the commitment? At the time, I was 17 years old and working as an apprentice electrician for $9 an hour. I was also working a lot of overtime to keep on top of rent and bills and to be able to feed myself. Living on an apprentice's wage wasn't easy, but I learnt a lot about money management. The most important thing I learnt about money: don't run out. Yep, that one's really important. I quickly learnt it wasn't enough to live pay cheque to pay cheque. I had to have money in the bank at all times in case my car broke down or some other unforeseen expense arose.

While I was excited about the audio hire business, the passion to make it work with my current situation wasn't there. I didn't have the capital, and I didn't have the time. Could I have made it work if I really wanted to? Possibly. But ideas are cheap, and I didn't have the passion or drive to follow through with the execution, so I moved on and took some important lessons with me.

So, was my audio hire idea crazy, genius, or just plain stupid? Honestly, I never really got to find out. But I did get a preview of what fully committing to an idea might look like, and, at that time, I wasn't ready for that sort of commitment. I wasn't in love with the problem I was trying to solve.

Biodegradable Plastic

Later, I started a business that developed a biodegradable plastic. The compound was designed to be used for lures but could also be adapted for netting and other items used in the fishing industry. On top of that, the plastic was harmless when ingested by sea life.

I'll admit, this idea was a little more exciting than the audio hire platform because it had the potential to make a real impact in the world. If our biodegradable plastic ended up in the ocean, it would break down naturally. If fish ate it, they would be fine. The product was a game changer, but I wouldn't be the one to steer it to success. While I had a great time running the business, my heart wasn't in it. I was already in the process of starting Tiliter, which I was much more passionate about, so I sold the IP (intellectual property) and moved on. Although I didn't take that particular idea all the way, I did put it out there so someone else could continue what I had started.

Want to Earn a Degree in Problem Solving? Start a band!

Before everything else, there was the band. As I mentioned, our band, Chasing Tuesday, was an acoustic duo that consisted of me and my best friend Chris. In those days, we were young and dumb enough to think that starting a band and touring the country wasn't a completely crazy thing to do. We were definitely passionate in the beginning, and we learnt a lot about business as we, with practically no money to our names, figured out how to create merch, produce music, and sell CDs (remember those?). Somehow, we had to fund all the touring, music production, gear purchasing, and other expenses that accompany being in a band. It isn't cheap, and money doesn't come easily. It really is a grind until you make it big – if you ever do.

We never went full-time with the band. Even when we were touring, we still worked regular jobs and had to get creative to make the scheduling work. At one point, we had an important gig coming up, but there was a problem. We lived in a share house and wouldn't get home from work until around 9 pm most nights, which was too late to make a lot of noise. So, we came up with a solution. We would grab our acoustic guitars, jump in the car, and drive to a secluded location. It was usually a park or car park somewhere away from residential areas. Once, we even ended up in the car park of the Chamber of Commerce. For hours, we would run through the set list, fine-tuning our performance until we felt we were ready for the gig. I can only imagine what anyone who happened to walk by must have thought. But we ended up putting on a great show, so it was well worth the effort.

Ultimately, we decided to step off the music path and pursue business. By then, I had practically earned a degree in problem solving, which would be invaluable in everything I did next. I hate to say it, but band life isn't as glamorous as it might seem. It's not all about the music or the gigs or the fame. Much like in business, each day comes with a new set of problems to solve. *How can we practise late at night without disturbing the peace? How can we get ourselves from gig to gig with minimal resources? How can we get from Sydney to Melbourne within a tight timeframe and be ready to play a show?* In the last example, we took advantage of a 24-hour gym, where we showered and got ready before the gig. To succeed in business – or in a band – you've got to be resourceful. You've got to think differently. You've got to be able to problem solve, day in, day out.

When your startup reaches the point of hiring staff, the number one thing you should look for in your candidates is problem solving skills. Why? Because you're going to meet problems on every step of the journey – we certainly did as a band and later as a startup – so you want people on board who can solve those problems. Makes sense, right?

As spirited young men, the band days were exciting. We didn't have a manager or an agent so everything that happened, *we* made it happen, earning an unofficial degree along the way. If we majored in problem solving, we minored in getting shit done, and the lessons we learnt and the experience we gained paved the way for future success.

THE FAIL FAST (OR LEARN FAST) MENTALITY

When starting businesses, entrepreneurs tend to adopt a fail-fast mentality. It's not so much about failing fast but more about testing an idea as quickly as possible to determine whether to stick with it or move on. Sometimes this mindset gets mistaken for a lack of focus, but that's not what it is. When we bounce from business to business, we're trying to find that all-important traction point. We want to reach our goals in the quickest and best way possible. If the traction point isn't there, we move on to the next idea.

Generally, an entrepreneur will have a million different ideas running through their mind. The key is deciding which ones to execute and which ones to toss aside. Ideally, we want to know whether an idea is crazy or genius at the earliest possible moment. We don't want to invest too much time, effort, or capital in a business that's too insane to succeed, but we also don't want to miss out on creating a possible unicorn, so we keep failing fast until we find traction.

When you're in the early stages of starting a business, failing – or succeeding – fast is crucial. Capital is limited; support may not be great, and customers aren't lining up to buy your product just yet. Therefore, you need to find out what works and what doesn't as quickly as possible. Like I said, it's more about learning fast than failing fast. When an idea doesn't succeed, you may not need to scrap it completely. Instead, you may be able to adapt, pivot, and take a different angle. If you're testing an idea and you're not hitting your numbers, you need to figure out how to get them trending in the right direction, which could mean completely changing course. I've seen businesses find success this way countless times.

A good example that comes to mind is Slack. The product started as a browser-based MMORPG (massively multiplayer online role-playing game) called *Glitch*. However, the game struggled to gain traction and build a large enough player base, causing the project to officially end in 2012. Although Glitch itself was gone for good, the game's chat functions were reworked into the app we now know as Slack. Slack Technologies, as I'm sure you know, went on to become a multi-billion-dollar company.[1]

At the time, pivoting to create a standalone chat app must have seemed completely crazy. How many people do you think saw the genius behind that idea early on? Not only were they attempting to salvage a tool from a defunct video game, but they were competing with all the other products in that space, which included Skype and several other instant messaging apps. As we know, the bold and somewhat questionable move paid off. Suddenly, Slack became one of the most successful products in the world, proving the genius behind the idea – and it all came from an epic failure.

HOW TO IDENTIFY A GENIUS IDEA (AND WEED OUT THE CRAZY ONES)

You might be asking, *How do I know if my idea is crazy or genius?* For obvious reasons, it's good to answer this question as soon as possible. You don't want to run too far with a concept that's too insane to succeed. Your time and energy would be better spent on an idea that could actually lead to a successful outcome.

I've made some seemingly crazy decisions over the years – for example, quitting my well-paying corporate job to start a business and later packing up my entire life to move overseas – but there's one key reason why these seemingly insane ideas succeeded: they were calculated. Yep, I wasn't making crazy choices, relying on luck to steer me to success. Instead, every step of the way was modelled and measured to a tee. *I* knew I wasn't crazy – I had the facts behind me – so it didn't matter what anyone else thought.

If you want to approach entrepreneurship with that same level of (relative) certainty, I've got great news for you: you can.

All you need to do is follow a simple yet powerful four-step process for identifying the genius ideas and weeding out the crazy ones:

1. Premortem

2. Circle of competence

3. Hedgehog concept

4. Feedback loops

Each model plays a critical part in the process, so let's discuss each one in detail and put you on the path to genius.

Premortem

When I was deciding whether or not to quit my corporate job, I sat down with my father, and we discussed all possible pitfalls, successes, outcomes, and major risks involved in starting a business. We even discussed financial planning, market research, and customer acquisition strategies.

Essentially, we created a premortem mental model, which is a technique used for imagining that a project has failed so you can work backwards to determine what might have caused that outcome. By doing this, you can identify potential pitfalls and take steps to avoid them before they become a problem.

The Premortem

Imagine failure, then work backwards.

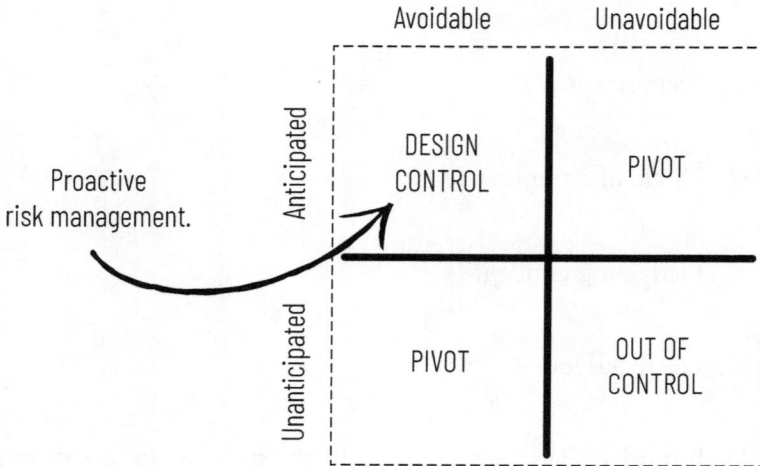

By the end of our conversation, I felt much more confident and prepared to take the leap into entrepreneurship, and I continued to apply this framework to every big decision, every major step of my journey. When you consider all possible futures, you learn pretty quickly whether your idea is crazy or potentially genius.

Circle of Competence

As my business grew, I realised there were things I was good at and things that were outside of my circle of competence. I noticed patterns in execution that directly related to expertise and knowledge within the business, which makes sense, right? You can't be a master of all trades. As we grew, we pursued opportunities outside of our core competencies, which led to less than successful outcomes.

However, by understanding our strengths and limitations, we were able to make better decisions about which opportunities to pursue and which to pass on. I quickly learnt that by staying within your circle of competence, you can reduce the risk of making costly mistakes and increase your chances of success.

The Circle of Competence

Identify your areas of expertise. Focus there.

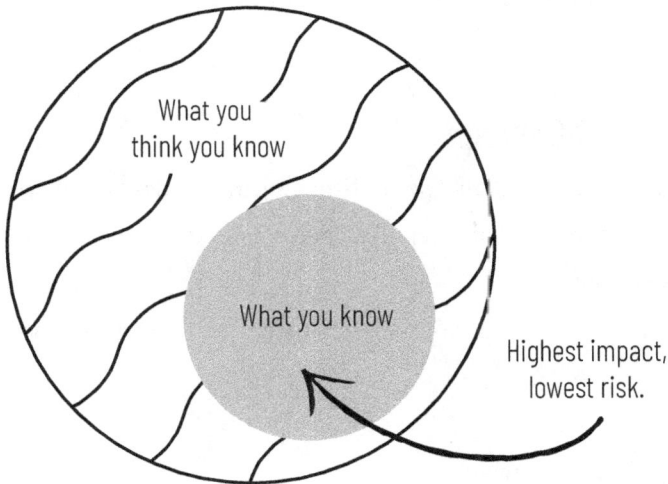

What you think you know

What you know

Highest impact, lowest risk.

Let me give you a real-world example. At one point, we had an opportunity to branch out into a new industry. At face value, the opportunity was amazing – a genius move! However, the more I analysed our expertise and tried to carve out a method of execution, the more I realised the risks were too high and many other factors were too unknown. Based on my analysis, I concluded that the idea fell into the crazy category, so we passed on the opportunity.

Years later, I learnt that multiple companies had taken up the challenge and ultimately failed, sinking a lot of time, energy, and money into trying to solve the problem. Looking back, we absolutely dodged a bullet with that one.

With the 'circle of competence' framework, you need to be okay with passing on a seemingly good opportunity if you can't envision a probable path to success. Sure, someone else might be able to make it happen, but knowing your own limitations and acting accordingly is vital to staying in the genius lane.

Hedgehog Concept

In his book, *Good to Great*, Jim Collins explains the hedgehog concept, a mental model that helps you determine where your focus should be.[2]

First, you should ask yourself three key questions about your business:

1. What are we passionate about?

2. What can we be the best in the world at?

3. What drives our economic engine?

The first circle – what you are passionate about – refers to the things that you love doing and bring you joy and fulfillment.

The Hedgehog Concept
Where all your energy should go.

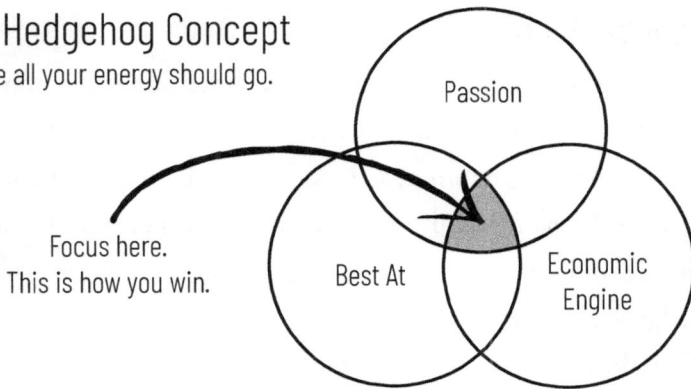

Passion

Focus here.
This is how you win.

Best At

Economic
Engine

The second circle – what you can be the best in the world at – refers to the things that you excel at and can do better than anyone else.

The third circle – what drives your economic engine – refers to the things that make you money and that you can sustainably earn profits from.

The intersection of these three circles is the area where your business should focus all its efforts and resources. It's where it can achieve the greatest success.

I once turned down an extremely lucrative contract because it didn't fit within this intersection. The pull to shift or dilute your company's focus can be difficult to resist, especially when there's money on the table, but if the move doesn't align with the hedgehog concept, you risk doing a bunch of things at an okay level instead of one thing amazingly. By using this framework, I was able to point my company's efforts towards the things we did best, which led to greater long-term profitability, growth, and sustainability. You can't do it all, so you might as well focus on what you excel at.

Feedback Loops

When using the three frameworks mentioned, I continually assess the outcomes, which is an essential part of the process. If I perform a premortem, I assess how it played out later. If I make a decision based on the circle of competence, I assess how that played out too. If I double down on an idea after using the hedgehog model – you guessed it – I assess how that played out. How do I do this? Feedback loops.

Feedback loops are critical for achieving, and maintaining, success. By continuously measuring and analysing performance metrics, you can identify areas for improvement and make informed decisions about how to optimise your operations. Importantly, you can determine whether you're heading down the path of crazy or genius. If you neglect to monitor progress and assess outcomes, you'll fail to both recognise emerging trends and rapidly respond to changes in the market or industry.

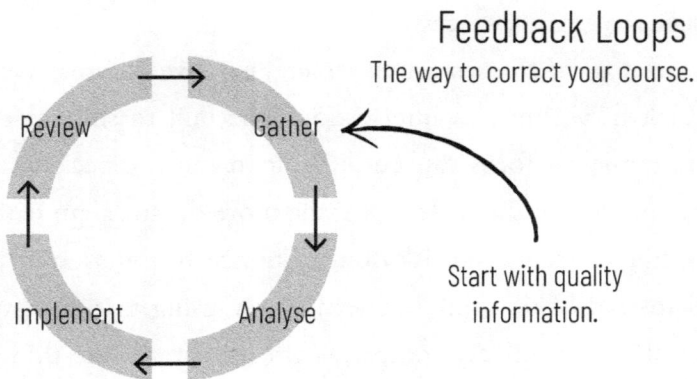

Feedback Loops
The way to correct your course.

Review

Gather

Implement

Analyse

Start with quality information.

I'll admit, even after using the premortem, circle of competence, and hedgehog concepts, I've been wrong – plenty of times! However, in almost every case, I was able to recognise my missteps through the feedback loop and correct course, creating comfort around the decision-making process.

By nature, entrepreneurs pursue bold and unconventional ideas that challenge the status quo, and it's hard to know whether a venture is crazy or genius until it either succeeds or fails. But, through mental models, you *can* stack the odds in your favour.

To me, crazy is making decisions on a whim. It's analysing outcomes and not knowing why they occurred. It's being unclear on the real goal. It's going along for the ride while chance, luck, fate – whatever you want to call it – does all the heavy lifting. It's going off a gut feeling that doesn't exactly inspire confidence in the people around you.

On the flip side, genius is approaching decision-making with logic, reasoning, and practicality, despite still pushing boundaries. We're entrepreneurs, remember? We still need to challenge the status quo. It involves the same perceived risks as the crazy approach, but it's not intuition guiding us – it's measurement, analysis, results. It's finding comfort when we're at our most uncomfortable.

In short, genius is calculated, modelled, measured.

So, is your idea crazy or genius? Honestly, you can never truly know until you witness the outcome.

1. Be calculated with your chaos. Essentially, 'trust the process'. Create solid frameworks you can rely on, like the four I mentioned, and ensure you lean on them.

2. Challenges don't stop. You have the same problems, just at a larger scale – from earning friends' support to investors, customers, suppliers, employees, and so on.

3. Find a drive that's sustainable. If you're relying on spite or fame or anything that isn't true to you, it won't be sustainable. You need to want to do this wholeheartedly.

4. Perception shifts with success. The same idea may be deemed crazy or genius based on the outcome.

5. Early validation is crucial. Quickly identifying whether an idea is viable can save significant resources.

6. Embrace your inner maverick. Innovating requires a bit of madness; knowing how to harness this is key.

7. Exercise resilience against doubt. Persistence in the face of scepticism can eventually win over critics and turn ideas into successes.

PHILOSOPHY

2

YOU CAN DO ANYTHING, BUT YOU CAN'T DO EVERYTHING

EARLY LIFE LESSONS FROM THE FARM

Growing up on a farm in Western Australia, I learnt a lot about hard work, sacrifice, and always having a plan. When you're relying on the land and your own labour to make a living and put food on the table, there's no room for slacking off. With no backup plan, my parents couldn't afford to stop working to raise us children, which meant we had to grow up fast. If the work didn't get done and we didn't have money coming in, we wouldn't have been able to eat. It was as simple as that. Fortunately, my parents were hard workers, and we never went without. They knew they couldn't do everything they wanted to do, so they chose their priorities wisely.

I didn't realise it at the time, but my parents sacrificed a lot for the family. Mum put her career on hold to raise us kids and work when she could, and Dad worked hard every day to put food on the table. Of course, we all pitched in and helped when we could, learning the value – and discomfort – of hard work earlier than we might have had we lived in the city. I didn't mind the labour at first. Every task had a purpose and was part of a larger plan. We always had to be thinking ahead and strategising to ensure that everything fell perfectly into place. Even though the day-to-day tasks kept us busy, we were constantly working towards future outcomes, and running a business is very much the same.

Whether working a farm or running a business, the small tasks matter. Each action you take, no matter how small, brings you a step closer to your goal. Typically, there's no rapid dash to the finish line. You get there one step, one decision, one action at a time. But those actions must be deliberate and serve a direct purpose. That's why having a strategy in place is important. Out of context, all those little tasks won't make a lot of sense, and you may find yourself asking, *Why am I even doing this?* People often get put off when they don't see instant results or create an immediate impact. However, when they finally take a step back after a year or two and review what they've done and how far they've come, they soon realise that all those small tasks add up to something big.

Similarly, when I step back and analyse my early life – from growing up on a farm to pursuing a football career – it's clear that every lesson I learnt, every decision I made, and every action I took led me to where I am today.

As entrepreneurs, we're often compelled to try to do it all and chase down every idea and business opportunity that presents itself. While you can do (almost) anything, you can't do everything. In this chapter, we'll discuss the importance of narrowing your focus, pushing forward with purpose, and working harder than the competition to stay in – and win! – the game.

THE ACCIDENT THAT ENDED MY FOOTBALL CAREER (AND ALMOST ENDED ME)

Early on, I decided I would have a career in sport, and for me football was always number one. Unfortunately, the closest high-level team to where I lived was a good four-hour drive away. I could have easily missed out on being involved in the elite scene when I was younger. Fortunately, however, my parents were very supportive, and we ended up doing two or three trips per week so I could continue to train, play, and try to build a career.

From about 14 years old, I played in state carnivals and frequently had conversations with recruiters and other clubs. By age 16, I was playing senior football and really getting exposed to the leadership and teamwork skills required to be a part of an elite team. I wasn't the most talented player, but I put in the work. In sport, business, and life, putting in the extra effort, really going above and beyond, goes a long way. My dream career as a professional footballer was unfolding before me, and I was on track to achieve my big life goal. But how often do things really go to plan?

I was 18 years old when I played my final game. We'd had a great season and were set to play to determine whether we would go straight to the grand final or have to play again the following week for another shot at the slot. Although I had played in a couple of grand finals, I had never won one, so I saw this as my big chance to finally be a part of a premiership-winning team. We had some amazing friends and people from the community behind us. Most importantly, we also had some amazing footballers. For us, the premiership was well within reach.

Now, I don't actually remember anything about the game. Everything I know comes from watching footage and hearing other people's accounts. Sometime during the third quarter, another player and I clashed heads, and I went down. I was fully out of it – and out of the game. After a couple of minutes, I was put on a stretcher and taken back to the club rooms. I didn't know who anyone was or what was happening, so I was taken directly to Westmead Hospital, not fully understanding the seriousness of the situation.

At the time, Westmead had the best neuroscience department in the state, so, after suffering a head injury, going there made sense. The medical staff did some scans, and I learnt I had a fractured skull. Apparently, one piece of bone was pressing against my brain, which was clearly a problem. Still, even though I was in the ICU, I don't think I fully understood the severity of my injury. But the people around me seemed to understand something I didn't, and their reactions gave me pause. Eventually, it was clear to me that I was dealing with much more than a simple bump to the head.

The support I received from the community was amazing. My coach quickly came to visit me in hospital to see how I was and let me know the club was behind me. On top of that, one of my all-time favourite footballers, Sam Butler from the West Coast Eagles, signed and sent me the headgear he had worn after suffering a concussion in one of his games. Receiving the support of someone I admired – and had never even met – was amazing and definitely helped lift my spirits. Perhaps a little too much.

In my mind, I would spend a couple of weeks recovering; then I would be back on the field. Looking back, I was too young and naive to fully grasp what was happening. At that age, we think we're invincible, and it takes a big event to change that belief. If a fractured skull and weeks in intensive care didn't convince me of my own mortality, nothing would. Once I moved out of the ICU and into standard care, I finally started to understand the seriousness of my injury. In time, I accepted that contact sports were now completely off the cards. I would never play football again.

Suddenly, my life's plan, my career, my very identity lay in ruins, never to be restored. I had grown used to being 'the guy who plays football' and without the game, I didn't know who I was anymore. I had been so focused on pursuing a career as a professional footballer that I hadn't stopped to consider what I would do if I could no longer follow that path.

Naturally, I was devastated, and I experienced an identity crisis of sorts. But the situation prompted me to rethink my philosophy on life, career, and business. I realised that my job, whatever it was, wasn't me – it wasn't my identity. While football, the club, and the community were a big part of my life, they weren't a part of me; I was a part of them. Once I made the separation, I felt much better about the future.

When running a startup, being able to separate yourself from the business is really important. You don't want to be too emotionally involved. I quite often see founders whose own identities are strongly tied to their business or product, which worries me from a mental health perspective. If something goes wrong – and let's be honest, things *will* go wrong – or the business fails, they might see the failure as a reflection of them. Clearly, it isn't the healthiest mindset to have, which is something entre-preneurs need to acknowledge and overcome as early as possible. You are not your company. You are not your product. Granted, to take your business to the next level, you'll need to put a big piece of yourself into it, but that doesn't mean your business should become your identity. If you can maintain a healthy level of separation, the big failures won't hit so hard, and you'll be able to keep moving forward much more easily.

My injury gave me an opportunity to reflect and ask the question: *What's next?* To top things off, my girlfriend also broke up with me. So, I had no football career, no girlfriend, and no idea what I was going to do with my life. What I did have was a lot of time on my hands, so I made the most of it, picking up the pieces, learning what I could, and putting conscious effort into thinking about what I wanted to do.

Interestingly, the more I thought about it, the more driven I became to do *something*. I was starting to get some momentum going, and momentum, as I'm sure you know, is really important. If you remain stationary, you won't get anywhere. You can't just sit around and wait for something to happen. It's like driving a car. Ideally, you should first have a destination in mind, but that's not always necessary. Sometimes a little exploration is needed. The important thing is that you start driving because as long as you do, you're going to end up *somewhere*. But how do you choose a destination or even a general direction? It all comes down to one crucial question: What are you passionate about? Understanding what you're *not* passionate about is also important. While you can be successful in a venture you don't have a great passion for, to build something from scratch, take it to the next level, and achieve the highest level of success, the passion has to be there.

After my injury, I spent a couple of years learning what I could, exploring different ideas, and really pushing myself to discover what I was passionate about now that sport was off the cards. During this time, I began to realise how important the people around us are. We're the product of our environment, and the people we surround ourselves with shape who we are. Having mentors who can help direct you in life is also important. In my search for a new purpose, I started reaching out to different people for advice. I was already receiving advice from some mentors organically, and I hadn't actually realised they were mentors until I began actively asking for their help.

After a lot of soul-searching, I found the path I wanted to take, and my entrepreneurial journey began.

A JOURNEY STARTS WITH ONE STEP AND CONTINUES WITH THE NEXT, AND THE NEXT, AND THE NEXT...

My parents were both entrepreneurial people. Aside from the farm, they ran various businesses over the years and were always trying to improve their situation. They knew that farming wasn't sustainable long-term. While we certainly could have survived on the farm, we couldn't have thrived, so my parents were always looking for other ways to build wealth and create more freedom for us all. Seeing them strategise, plan ahead, and take deliberate action towards reaching their goals instilled that same mentality in me, which helped a great deal on my entrepreneurial journey.

Through my parents, I learnt the value of planning ahead but also the importance of focusing on the here and now. It's easy to get ahead of ourselves and start trying to do too much or rush the process. As long as you have a clear goal and are taking the right steps to get there, you're on the right track. When you try to take on too much for whatever reason, there's a good chance you're going to do several things averagely rather than one thing spectacularly.

When starting a business, you need to be deliberate in your actions, and every action must be done with intent. Simply trying to coast by and see where you end up is one of the worst things you can do. If you don't have a goal, your first step is to make one. Once your target is clear, you can start taking all the tiny steps that will get you there.

During the COVID pandemic, I took up golf. It's not football, but it's a challenging sport that I quickly grew to love. In golf, a lot of players will take a swing, aiming for a fairly large target area. The problem with that is that when they miss, they often miss big. If, instead, they were to aim for a smaller, more distinct target, suddenly even their misses would be a lot closer to the goal. You're better off narrowing your focus and making your target as clear as possible. Doing this, you'll have much more success. The same logic applies to creating a strategy and setting goals in business. When you have a clear target, even if you miss, the miss won't be as catastrophic as it might have been if you were aiming too wide. In reality, if you still manage to miss big, you may have picked the wrong target, and it's time to learn from the failure and choose a new direction. Small misses are easy to correct. Big misses require a complete rethink of the strategy that got you there – because something clearly isn't working.

If you do miss big, it could also be that you tried to shoot too far too soon. Most successful companies get to where they are in the style of a marathon rather than a sprint: one foot in front of the other, one decision after the next, over and over again until they arrive at the finish line. Rarely is it a quick sprint to success.

RISK ASSESSMENT AND REACHING NEW HEIGHTS

When I talk about the importance of having a clear target, I'm not saying you shouldn't try to think big, create lofty goals, and push yourself – and others – to meet them. However, you do need to be calculated and realistic in your approach.

Firstly, you can ignore the boundaries. They aren't real. The playing field is whatever you decide it is. When we overreach and really push ourselves, sometimes we get surprising results. Often, it's better to be a little too ambitious than not ambitious enough. But, ultimately, it's all about understanding the risks and deciding whether the big overambitious swing is worth it or not.

Growing up in the country, I learnt a lot about risk assessment and mitigation. Most of the time, we were dealing with physical risks. Is the path ahead safe? Is there a snake in the grass? Are we operating our machinery safely? When working on a rural property, an incorrect risk assessment can lead to injury or even death. So, we learn to spot risks early, but we also learn when to take risks – and sometimes we get it wrong.

When I was young, I was riding my bike around the property, thinking about how cars have seatbelts. Clearly, my bike was missing a very important safety feature, so I made a seatbelt using a rope. I thought I was a genius until Dad explained that I had actually created more risk. "If you crash your bike," he said, "you'll be attached to it, and you won't be able to control your landing." He was right, of course, and that's why bikes don't have seatbelts. Sometimes we need an experienced mentor to point out the risks for us.

In business, the risks aren't usually physical, although health and safety issues do exist. Most of the time, we're dealing with financial repercussions if a strategy goes sideways or a plan doesn't pan out. But if you want to truly innovate and be a standout in your industry, a little overreach and a few risky manoeuvres may be necessary.

My bike seatbelt (rope tied to a bike) may not have been my best invention, but, looking back, it's clear that I had a bit of an inventor's streak in me at a young age. Fortunately, my product design – and risk assessment – skills improved over time.

RESOURCEFULNESS IS YOUR GREATEST RESOURCE

Resourcefulness is one of the most important skills you can cultivate in yourself and your team. On the farm, no task was ever too big, and no problem was without a solution. If something had to be done, we had to find a way to do it. It was as simple as that.

Some of my friends who grew up in the city typically hire someone if something needs doing that's outside of their immediate skill set. Either that, or the task just doesn't get done. Whereas, growing up in the country, we had to be resourceful. A lot of the time, we couldn't afford to hire someone to do specialised work and even if we could, there wasn't always someone in the area qualified to do the work. So, if something needed doing, we always found a way to do it. If we needed a tool we didn't have – or that didn't exist – we would make it. We often had to come up with unconventional solutions to difficult problems, which is a *big* part of being an entrepreneur and startup founder. You're not always going to have the tools you need, and coming up with the best solutions to near-impossible problems requires a lot of creativity and, often, a small streak of insanity, too.

My grandparents were also very resourceful people. On two occasions, they persuaded me to holiday at their farm in WA. The first time, I spent the entire two weeks out in a paddock picking beans. It wasn't my idea of a holiday and more resembled the backpacker experience – but my grandparents were smarter than that. Hiring backpackers still costs money. However, persuading a family member to spend their entire holiday picking beans costs practically nothing. At the end of each day, I was wrecked. The second time my grandparents invited me for an extended stay at the farm, I was silly enough to think this time was actually going to be a holiday. By then, I had my electrical licence, and coincidentally my grandparents needed some electrical work done. So, I spent my two-week holiday wiring their shed. In return, I learnt another valuable lesson about being resourceful, working on a budget, and taking advantage of – or should I say *utilising* – family. It was essentially a continuation of my informal education, particularly that minor in 'getting shit done'.

HONING YOUR COMPETITIVE EDGE

When I was playing football, in reflection, I wasn't the most talented player. However, to make up for my lack of natural talent, I worked very, very hard. If I slacked off even a bit, there was no way I would have kept up with the more gifted players in the league. Until my accident, I put everything into football. My focus was on just one thing: getting better at the game. If I had put my attention and energy into achieving too many different goals, I wouldn't have been able to hone that competitive edge that comes from a singular focus and utter dedication to doing the work. Remember, you can do anything, but you can't do everything.

As an entrepreneur, you'll likely begin your journey as the underdog, especially when creating a startup from scratch. If you want to compete with the bigger players, you must have a clear focus and be prepared to work harder than the competition. It's the only way to catch up to – and eventually surpass – competitors that already have an advantage, whether that be financial, talent, or something else. Focus is important. If you're constantly changing your mind about what you're trying to accomplish, success will be difficult to achieve. Of course, you should be flexible and be able to pivot when necessary, but, at some stage – sooner rather than later – you need to double down and commit to a long-term strategy.

In the startup space, you could have a business with millions of dollars of funding and hundreds of employees competing with another that has next to no funding and only a handful of employees. It may not seem like a fair and level playing field, and, in many ways, it's not, but life rarely is fair. During my football career, I didn't let the more gifted players put me off. Instead, I used them for fuel and inspiration, and you need to take the same approach in business. So, when you can't compete financially, how *can* you compete? It basically comes down to mindset, culture, and hard work. If you're more passionate and driven than the competition, it's going to reflect in your products and services, and suddenly you're able to compete in a meaningful way. When you really work to understand the problem you're trying to solve, you're going to come up with better solutions. In contrast, a business that doesn't take the time to thoroughly investigate the problem will generally fall short with the solution it provides. Well-financed companies often think they can fall back on superior resources if they don't quite get it right. It's just like sport. When a player doesn't feel like they *need* to win, they're not going to work as hard. Whereas, for someone who's risking it all, losing isn't an option. They *must* win, or it's all over. They have no choice but to put everything into achieving success. Desperation can be a powerful motivator.

In both business and sport, there are always people who are working harder. There are always people who are pushing things to the next level. They're the people who become the elite of the elite and are prepared to battle through the hard times to reach the highest levels of success. Generally, in business, the company that works the hardest is going to win. If you're persistent and consistently putting in the hard work, you will eventually reap the rewards. Talent and capital will only get you so far. The businesses that make the biggest impact are those that utilise what they've got and make up the difference with hard work and unwavering determination.

Not everyone can raise millions of dollars in funding, but anyone can choose to put in the extra effort to gain a competitive edge.

HOW DO YOU KNOW WHEN TO BAIL ON A BUSINESS, CAREER, OR IDEA?

When I fractured my skull playing football, I had no choice but to give up the sport. It was 100 percent clear to me that I had to bail on that career and find a new path forward. Often, however, the signs that suggest it's time to move on aren't so clear.

When running a business or attempting to get an idea off the ground, how do you know when you're walking into a dead end? How do you know it's time to bail on that particular goal and try something else? Quitting feels bad. It's practically admitting defeat, right? But if you refuse to bail on a bad idea because you fear failure, you could end up doing a lot more damage to yourself mentally and financially in the long run. Besides, every failure is a lesson that will help you achieve future success. So, knowing when to bail on a bad idea is vital.

If you can't trust your own judgement, external input can help clarify the situation. That's why it's important to have mentors, coaches, or other people around you who are willing to be honest and have the knowledge and experience required to offer sound advice. You don't want to be surrounded by a bunch of yes men (or women). You need people who are willing to tell it like it is. If all of your mentors are telling you the same thing – for example, an idea isn't worth pursuing or continuing to pursue – you should probably listen. The same applies to life in general. If you continually receive the same advice, it might be time to start taking it seriously and act on it. It's basically the wisdom of the crowd – just make sure the crowd *is* actually wise before you take its advice.

Additionally, you should add an internal aspect to your analysis. For example, setting goals and, importantly, reviewing them regularly will help you understand whether you're on the right track. Are your internal numbers and metrics meeting expectations and aligning with your objectives? If you don't measure, you might not know that you're failing – or succeeding, for that matter. If external input is telling you something, your internal metrics will either confirm or disprove it.

In short, if you want to know if it's time to bail on an idea or keep pushing forward, a combination of internal and external information should help you arrive at a clear conclusion. With that said, the answers you receive won't always align. However, as long as you're correctly measuring and interpreting your internal metrics, they should have the final word. The numbers never lie.

NATURE VS. NURTURE – WHAT SHAPES AN ENTREPRENEUR?

My father was really good with his hands. If he wanted to do or make something, he would just do it. He didn't need help, and he certainly didn't need permission. If he saw a problem, he found a way to solve it. Once, we needed a trailer, but do you think Dad just went out and bought one? Not a chance. Why would he waste the money when we had a heap of perfectly good scrap metal lying around? So, instead of buying a trailer, he designed and built his own.

Clearly, I was exposed to the entrepreneurial mindset early. Dad's DIY mentality transferred to me, and, from bands to business, I never let a problem get in the way of continual progress. If an issue could be solved, I could solve it. Often, things aren't as impossible as they seem at first glance.

Playing highly competitive sport at a young age also shaped the person I became. I recall one occasion when 300 of us would-be AFL superstars were sitting and listening as a head selector from one of the teams gave a speech. "Look around," he said. "Statistics tell us that the best-case scenario is that only five to ten of you will make it through." At the time, that seemed insane to me. We all thought we were going to make it. We were all putting in the effort. We were all making major sacrifices. But he was right, and his statement brought me and many others back down to earth. If we were going to succeed, we couldn't just put in the effort and sacrifice a lot. We had to give it all and sacrifice *everything*.

In business and sport, no one simply coasts through to the elite level. That day, hearing such a daunting statistic from the head selector was the spur I needed to start working harder than the next guy to ensure I would beat the odds and secure a place in the top ten. So, at an early age, I learnt the value of going all-in on a goal, which absolutely shaped me into the entrepreneur I later became.

I truly do believe we're the products of our environments. Regardless of your personality or who you think you are, the people you surround yourself with will shape the person you become.

From growing up on a farm, to playing football at an elite level, to moving out of home at age 17, trying to make ends meet with a $9 an hour job, to keeping a touring band afloat on a shoestring budget – those early life experiences taught me the lessons I needed to learn and gave me the tools I needed to acquire to succeed in the startup space.

While I'm sure there was a fair bit of nature involved, I can't discount how much of an impact the people, places, and events in my life had in shaping the man and entrepreneur I eventually became.

NOT EVERYONE GETS TO EXPERIENCE FARM LIFE

Now, I'm not saying that everyone should grow up on a farm and that a rural upbringing is always an advantage, although it definitely was for me. If you didn't have a childhood full of hard labour, risky situations, and creative problem-solving, don't stress. You can put yourself through a boot camp of sorts in adulthood. How? By getting out there and doing something.

Nowadays, there are a lot of educational resources out there: books, podcasts, articles, videos – the list goes on. Being in this era of information is great. But how do you dissect it all and figure out what's relevant to you? By *doing*. Getting out there and trying different things is really important. Don't be afraid to fail. Don't be scared of making mistakes. The more you do, the more you'll learn about yourself and the world.

There are some amazing people out there who have done some awesome things, and they often talk about the path they took and the guidelines you should follow, but their advice may not suit you, your personality, or your objectives. You need to get out there and experience things for yourself to find out what works and what doesn't work for *you*. Using the principles of others is a great starting point, but you need to get out there, test the advice of experts, and form your own conclusions. That, of course, includes the advice in this book. There's no set way to do something, but there are ways that have worked well for others and could work for you too – or not. That's for you to figure out.

In academia, you receive a lot of information about what works, what doesn't, what's true, what's not, but these principles and conclusions don't always hold up once you step out into the real world. That's why taking action is important. The more you do, the more you'll know. Failure, in that sense, is actually success in disguise.

KEY TAKEAWAYS FROM CHAPTER 2

1. Know whether something is working or not. Make conscious decisions to double down on what works and drop what doesn't.

2. Find a really strong reason to win. All of your experiences and your skill set help form your competitive edge.

3. Focus on strategic priorities. Spreading yourself too thin can dilute efforts and hinder progress.

4. Align actions with goals. Ensure every task moves you towards your broader objectives.

5. Understand the value of hard work. Success in entrepreneurship, as on a farm, requires consistent focused effort.

6. Sacrifice is inevitable. Prioritising certain goals often means setting aside others.

YOU CAN DO ANYTHING, BUT YOU CAN'T DO EVERYTHING

PHILOSOPHY

3

INDECISION WILL KILL YOU

FAILING TOWARDS SUCCESS

Call them setbacks, hiccups, learning opportunities – however you label your failures, it's important to make sure they're moving you towards your goal and not in the other direction. So, how do you ensure you're failing forward? You need to have a destination in mind. That is, you must be clear on your end point to ensure that every action you take brings you closer to the success you envision, even when those actions don't achieve the desired results.

Now, I'm not saying that failure itself should ever be the goal. I've heard a lot of people say, "It's okay to fail." And it is – but it also isn't. When you're running a startup, failure isn't an option. That's not to say that setbacks won't occur, but you certainly shouldn't seek them out. Instead, you should be aiming to make the best decisions possible at any given time. You can't afford to get reckless. Your mindset and any actions you take should be geared towards success. Yes, setbacks are inevitable, and some may feel like catastrophic failures. But if you're clear on your direction, each setback will actually be a step forward, pushing you closer to your goal. Knowing what not to do is just as important as knowing what works.

The key to failing gracefully – and productively – is to accept the failure and figure out how to avoid the same misstep in the future. What went wrong? What could you have done differently? How will you address the failure both internally and externally? This is where a lot of companies get it wrong. Often, when they fail or make a mistake, they try to put a spin on it. There's always an excuse, especially when a failure has major consequences, like in the event of a serious data breach. If you don't do a deep dive into your failures, you'll never learn from them, and you'll never earn the confidence of your customers, your staff, or your peers.

When an idea or action is unsuccessful – success is always the goal, right? – it's time to perform a root cause analysis and determine what went wrong. Using the data breach example again, the companies that are open about what happened are the ones that gain back public trust. Whereas those that shirk responsibility – "It's not our fault! We did everything we could" – lose a lot of respect and struggle to regain their public standing. Think about it. If you purchase a car that has a manufacturing defect, which company would you trust and respect more: the one that admits the fault and fixes it free of charge or the one that denies any wrongdoing and refuses to address the issue? I know who I would choose.

So, acknowledging and analysing your failures not only gives you the opportunity to understand what went wrong, but it also helps build trust and respect within and outside the company. You can't control every outcome, but you *can* choose how you react to a setback or mistake.

You won't, of course, learn anything or get anywhere if you're not prepared to make the decisions required to move you forward. Some decisions will end in failure, but every choice you make has the potential to be a step towards success. In this chapter, we'll discuss effective leadership in the face of setbacks, the power of being decisive, and the epic failure that almost ruined me and my business.

LEAD THROUGH FAILURE, NOT TO IT

When you have an end point in mind, every failure – and success, for that matter – becomes clear. In most cases, an action that doesn't achieve the desired result is the victim of poor execution. The idea itself may be sound; however, you may need to perform a deep analysis to determine how to execute in a way that produces a better outcome.

As a leader, you need to be clear on your objectives up-front. When you have a strategy or roadmap designed to get you to your destination, recognising, analysing, and utilising a setback becomes much easier. If you don't know where you're trying to go, you may not even recognise a failure when it occurs, which is a really counterproductive way to operate.

An effective leader knows as much about what not to do as they do about what to do, and all that comes from experience. The more you encounter setbacks and success, the more adept you become at avoiding the former and achieving the latter. If you're hesitant to make decisions because you're scared of failure, I'm sorry, but you'll never get anywhere. Success should always be the goal, but a good leader knows how to guide people through failure when it occurs. Why? Because they always have the destination in mind.

DEATH BY INDECISION – WHAT A TRAGIC WAY TO DIE!

Running a startup is a fast-paced experience and if you're not keeping up with the frenzy, you could end up wasting a lot of money, whether that's your own or investors' capital. Every moment you spend *not* making a decision is money, resources, and mental clarity burnt. When you sit in stagnation, things start to get cloudy. You get so used to sitting around, wallowing in indecision, that the right decisions become harder to identify, and decisiveness in general becomes a foreign state of mind.

In my experience, indecision is one of the biggest startup killers. If you take too long to make a decision and take action, you'll quickly see the market and your competitors move ahead of you, and you'll struggle to catch up. When we fear failure, indecision can become a protective measure. You can't fail if you don't do anything, right? But if you refuse to make the call, you never learn what's right and wrong, what works and what doesn't. You actually make failure more likely in the long run.

In business, few things are worse than stagnation. Even if you make the wrong decision, at least you then *know* it was the wrong decision, and you can now take steps to make the right one. Making a decision is progress, no matter the outcome. Of course, making the right decisions as often as possible is preferable, but a misstep will bring you closer to success than refusing to take any step at all. Sometimes, making the wrong decision is simply the best way to get to the right one.

Once again, every decision you make, every action you take should be in the spirit of reaching your larger goal. You're not just arbitrarily deciding to do this or that and seeing where you end up; you're taking decisive steps towards your objective. Ideally, every decision you make should be as impactful as possible. That doesn't mean you need to change the world with every choice, but every action should have clear intent behind it. Where are you trying to go? What are you trying to achieve? There should be no room for doubt.

IT'S ALL ABOUT TIMING

When executing any idea, timing is essential. The businesses that perform well understand trigger points and plan their activities around them. For instance, you might decide to start raising capital, and the trigger point is that you're about to bring on a new customer, meaning investors would be getting a great deal if they invest *now*. So, if you time your funding rounds right, investing seems more attractive, and you're more likely to get that magic 'yes' from investors.

Every move you make should be calculated in this way. You should always be asking, "What's the ideal timing?"

Another example is linking project timelines to remuneration reviews. When you have major projects finishing right before remuneration, you motivate employees to perform because they want a pay rise. On top of that, when a project is complete, the results are clear, and you know whether a reward is justified. And if a project is overdue and not going well, you can take that into consideration too. If, on the other hand, you're only halfway through a project when remuneration rolls around, you don't really have any quantifiable metrics on which to base a decision. Is a pay rise justified or not? It becomes more of a guessing game when, ideally, you want everything to be as quantifiable as possible when making any decision.

Timing is especially important when it comes to releasing products, features, marketing, media – pretty much anything. You can't just put something out when *you* decide and expect to get the best results. Before you release anything, you need to understand how the market is behaving and determine the best timing. For example, if you release a bunch of media during, say, federal budget week, you're probably not going to get a lot of eyes on you because there's something bigger happening. When is your audience in the best position to pay attention to *you*? It's all about timing.

Everything you do should be part of a carefully considered timeline. If you mistime something important, you risk taking the wind out of your sails, losing momentum, and wasting an opportunity that could otherwise have been a big win.

For example, I've seen startups try to raise capital over the Christmas period, which, as I'm sure you can imagine, is a tough undertaking. Most people take breaks during this time; many businesses shut down, and you'll struggle to get anyone's attention or interest. If you're keen to run out of money and go bust, raising capital over the holiday period is a great way to do it. I've seen it happen, and, in most cases, it's easily avoidable. That's why timing is so important in every aspect of business. When every decision you make is perfectly timed, all you need to worry about is making the *right* decisions.

HOW DO YOU KNOW IF YOU MADE THE RIGHT CALL?

So, how do you know whether you made the right call or fucked up completely? Sometimes, a wrong decision will be glaringly, unavoidably, unquestionably obvious. Other times, the answer may not be so clear. That's why metrics are important. When you're measuring the right things, there should be little doubt in your mind whether an action is achieving the desired results.

One decision that often comes up in business has to do with partnerships. Do you go into partnership with someone else? Or do you continue to go it alone? Let's say you do decide to take the partnership route. How do you know if you've made the right decision? Your metrics will tell you – that's how. Perhaps the numbers indicate that you've stalled and aren't getting where you wanted to go. Maybe your partners didn't have the reach or resources you first thought; therefore, they aren't providing the value you expected. At that point, you'll likely need to make the decision to end the partnership. If you don't measure your progress and continue to analyse your decisions, you could spend years not realising that you made the wrong call. So, assessing your decisions once you've made them is just as important as being decisive.

If you're still hesitant to embrace the power of decision-making, I want you to consider this: When you fail to make decisions in a timely manner, who's actually controlling what you do? If you're sitting around, waiting for others or outside influences – customers, the market, the media, whoever – to make your decisions for you, you're no longer in control of your own destiny. Instead, you're allowing others to steer you in a direction that's unlikely to take you where you really want to be. The most successful businesses control their own destinies. When you submit to indecision, it's the equivalent of jumping on a random bus and hoping it goes somewhere close to where you want to go. However, when you're running a business, you can choose to drive the bus, which means you can take it anywhere you please, as long as you follow the road rules and don't hit any pedestrians along the way.

GOT A DESTINATION? USE A MAP

When making decisions, it's important to ensure they're moving you towards your objective. That means measuring and analysing your progress in relation to your ultimate goal.

Without a clear destination in mind and a solid plan to get there, you could end up taking a route that moves you further and further away from where you want to be. To compensate, you may even inadvertently start to change your goal, moving the goalposts to align with the new direction you're headed, which may not align with you, your values, or your true objective.

On the other hand, when you make decisions that correspond to your overall goal, you take a more linear – and much quicker – path to your destination. If you do happen to stray from the ideal path, you should aim to get back on track as soon as possible.

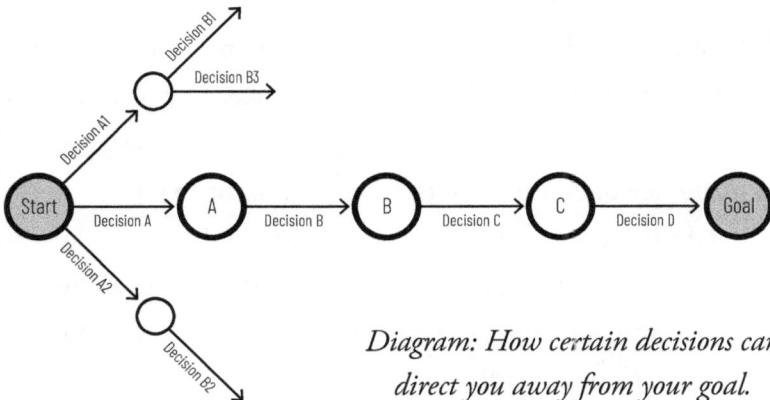

Diagram: How certain decisions can direct you away from your goal.

For example, if you make a decision that puts you on the wrong route, your next decision should point you back in the right direction. The dotted line in the following diagram illustrates my point.

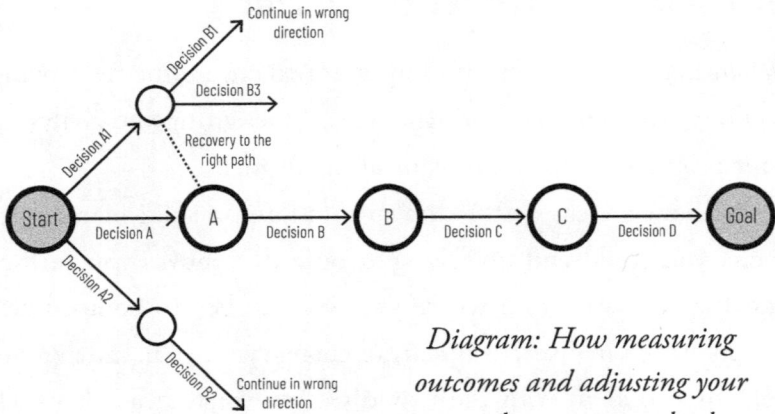

Diagram: How measuring outcomes and adjusting your approach can put you back on the right path.

Recovering from a misguided decision is like recovering from a poor shot in golf. If you're in trouble, it's rare that a miracle shot will save the day. Instead, you should aim to knock the ball back onto the fairway to give yourself the best opportunity of making it to the green. The alternative likely involves a lot of desperate strokes through trees, roughs, and other hazards, with no guarantee of ever getting to where you want to go.

If a decision puts you on the fastest path to the green – or your goal – you've likely made the right one. The key is to measure and assess the outcome of each stroke – or action – you take and adjust your game accordingly.

1. Sometimes recovery shots are more important than your original shot. Creating a step-by-step map and ensuring you're minimising risk and not going offcourse is incredibly important.

2. Link your trigger points in business – for example, product, raising capital, PR, and engineering – together. Timing these things can mean the difference between failing and succeeding. Even if on their own these things are amazing, they need to fit a viable timeline.

3. Decisiveness drives momentum. Making decisions, even if not perfect, moves you forward.

4. Learn from every decision. Each choice, right or wrong, provides valuable insights.

5. Avoid paralysis by analysis. Overthinking can lead to missed opportunities and stagnation.

6. Favour action over perfection. It's better to act and adjust than to wait for the perfect decision.

7. Don't stand still for too long. Sure, use your time to assess and understand but if you're stagnant for too long, you'll begin to lose momentum, which leads us to the next chapter...

PHILOSOPHY
4

MOMENTUM IS YOUR 'YES' MESSAGE

A STEEP CLIMB TO THE TOP

When it comes to explaining momentum in business, I like the old analogy about pushing a boulder up a hill. In the beginning, you're pushing hard, but you only seem to be climbing one laboured step at a time. However, as you reach the crest of the hill and the terrain starts to level out, your task becomes a little easier. Finally, you reach the very top, and suddenly the boulder starts to roll on its own, gaining momentum as it bowls down the other side of the hill.

You could apply this analogy to a lot of different things in life, but it works perfectly for business. No matter how difficult things seem right now, if you keep pushing, you will eventually reach a point where progress feels relatively effortless. However, that initial climb up the hill is *really* difficult, and it's no wonder that so many people give up before they reach the top.

Momentum is your 'yes' message, a sign that you're on the right track. In this chapter, we'll discuss maintaining momentum, identifying your target market, and choosing the right mentors to guide you on your journey. We've made it this far together, so let's keep the momentum going.

SIGNS OF A MOMENTUM SHIFT

In the beginning, before you've reached the top of the hill, the signs that indicate you're gaining momentum may not be obvious. Of course, the numbers will generally tell you how you're going, but you may notice other indicators of a momentum shift before the metrics give it away.

An often-overlooked sign that you're picking up speed is a shift in the internal culture of the business. Suddenly, people are more motivated, insightful, and willing to think and act ahead of even where you're thinking. While previously everything seemed forced, now everyone is working enthusiastically towards the same goal. They recognise the possibilities and understand what the business is all about. They resonate with the company values, and they're excited to make things happen.

As the founder of the business, you'll notice some of the burden of leadership starting to disperse. Suddenly, people are coming to you with exceptional ideas that absolutely align with your vision and bring you closer to your goal. They *get it*. They're getting things done before you've even thought to ask. And once you have that internal momentum happening, it won't be long until it seeps through to the outside, where you'll really start to notice the shift.

Naturally, you should always be measuring your progress whenever possible, whether internally or externally. In the beginning, a lot of businesses neglect to use tracking tools of any kind and simply rely on anecdotal evidence to determine how they're travelling. If they *think* something is going well, they *say* it is, even if they don't have the data to back it up. Or they might cite numbers they believe signify momentum when, in fact, they suggest the opposite.

For instance, traditionally, if a startup is hiring more people, you might think the business is doing quite well. It appears as though they're gaining momentum. However, bringing more people on board isn't necessarily a measure of success. Needing to hire more people could indicate that the business isn't running efficiently, is falling behind, and may not be pointed in the right direction. Of course, this isn't always the case, but you need to be careful about what metrics you use to measure momentum because you might be misinterpreting the story the numbers are telling.

If you truly are gaining momentum, you should be able to prove it to the external crowd with the right metrics. But once you finally do crest that hill, there will be no doubt in anyone's mind that a serious shift has occurred.

MOMENTUM DOESN'T MAINTAIN ITSELF

As entrepreneurs, we're always looking ahead. Gaining momentum in the present is great, but we don't have the luxury of spending too much time in the here and now. If we're not considering the next steps, we risk losing the momentum we've already built.

In a well-designed business, you'll have people whose job it is to maintain that momentum by improving current products, keeping customers on board, considering future products, and attracting new customers. All these things are about maintaining and increasing the momentum you've already built.

The problem is, success isn't always a linear path. In business, there will be good times, and there will be tough times. To maintain momentum, you need to know how to keep a company alive during the tough times and thriving in the good times. During a difficult period, you may lose some momentum, but you shouldn't come to a complete stop. The key is to plan for every situation so there are no surprises.

Personally, I like to create three financial plans: one for if everything is amazing, another for a more realistic and likely scenario, and another for if everything goes to shit and the walls start crumbling around me. Financially, the middle ground is where you'll likely end up, but your business may slip into the amazing or terrible zones from time to time, so you need to plan for them.

When your business is thriving, you don't want to waste the advantage. I've noticed two key issues that ruin momentum in times of success: complacency and greed. When a business is thriving, sometimes the people at the top don't believe innovation or improvement should be a big focus anymore. They go from a 'let's change the world' mindset to 'if it ain't broke, don't fix it'. But just because something ain't broke, it doesn't mean you can't improve it. Where would we be as a civilisation if we stopped trying to innovate?

When your business is thriving, you should be raising money, even if you don't need it right there and then. If tough times do roll around, at least you'll have some capital to fall back on, and you may not have to make as many sacrifices, which means you can keep the momentum going.

As mentioned, greed is another issue successful entrepreneurs face. Don't fall into that trap. When things are going well, you may feel compelled to raise prices to unrealistic levels or push the company in a direction that's more profit-driven than product-driven. While such decisions may generate short-term rewards, you're potentially sacrificing any long-term trust you've built with your audience, which is much more valuable than making a quick buck, right?

If, however, the walls do start falling down around you, you need to be prepared. What can you do to maintain momentum? Do you need to pull back on certain projects to focus on those that will keep the company alive? Do you need to make short-term sacrifices for long-term survival? Ideally, you should know what actions you need to take well before you need to take them.

In business, you always need to be thinking several moves ahead. Out of context, the next step may not make a lot of sense. However, sometimes your overall strategy will demand that you make a few, let's say, interesting decisions to get where you ultimately want to go. For example, the first product you release may not be your main offering in the future. It may just be a gateway to the next level, but it helps get that initial momentum happening; then you can maintain it in other ways.

Essentially, if you're customer-centric, providing value, thinking ahead, planning for all outcomes, and seeking continuous improvement, you won't have too much trouble maintaining the momentum you've built.

FIND THIS AS SOON AS POSSIBLE (PRODUCT-MARKET FIT)

When it comes to momentum, finding your product-market fit as soon as possible is crucial. Once you've nailed this, you can double down and really start pushing that boulder up the hill. At that point, you can start to invest in more long-term ideas and activities because you've proven your concept in the short-term. You don't want to invest too much time, money, and effort into the business until you've identified the ideal product-market fit. But once you have, it's game on!

When determining your target market, there are no secret paths or special shortcuts. In most cases, you'll be dealing with the typical startup scenario, and the tried and true methods are your best bet.

Firstly, you'll want to talk to as many people as possible, gather as much information as you can, and keep researching until you have a pretty good picture of your target market. Next, you'll need to actually try selling your product or service and start collecting numbers. Are people buying the product? How much does customer acquisition cost? Is the product profitable? Is it living up to its value proposition and meeting customer needs? Are there any barriers? Are customers receiving ROI? If you put genuine effort into understanding the customer buying journey, you should know whether you've found the right product-market fit or not.

Sometimes, the product you're planning to sell won't exist. Yet. I'm not talking about a scam, either. Before building your product, you may be waiting on money from pre-orders to finance that part of the process. Due to the popularity of crowdfunding, many businesses are now able to simultaneously gauge interest *and* fund the creation of a product before they've even built anything. Granted, you'd need to have a pretty solid concept and be able to instil a good amount of confidence in your audience to be successful taking this route, but the model certainly works when done well.

If people *are* willing to pay for a product before it exists – as long as you can follow through on all your promises – you know you're onto a winner.

CHOOSING THE RIGHT MENTORS

Let's be honest – most young entrepreneurs are inexperienced, and they're going to make more mistakes than someone who has been in the game for a while. However, you don't need to blindly walk into setback after setback when there's a simple way to determine whether you're making the right decision or not: utilise good mentors.

I can't overstate the value of having the support of someone – actually, multiple people – who are experienced in many different areas of business and life. You can't know everything, and there are plenty of people who have already been where you are now. So, why not utilise them?

While the value of having good mentors is clear, you might be asking: "How do I go about finding the right people to support me on my journey?" As always, strategy is key. Firstly, you need to do a deep analysis and really try to understand where your knowledge gaps are, both in a personal and business sense. If you can't hire someone to fill those gaps, you need a mentor who can share their expertise, guide you in the right direction, and identify any potential hazards before they become a major problem.

Once again, it all comes down to setting goals and having that end point in mind. If you don't know what you're trying to do, you won't understand what you need to know, and you'll end up either approaching the wrong mentors or failing to learn anything relevant. Ideally, you want all learnings and development to be impactful. The more unsure you are about your direction and overall objective, the broader the advice you seek will need to be, which lessens potential impact. However, when you know and understand your goals intimately, you can approach the right mentors, ask the right questions, and in turn receive the right advice.

For instance, if you've never managed people before and you're planning to build a team of, say, 200 people, you're going to need the guidance of someone with management experience. The key here is to *know* that building a large team is one of your goals so you can then seek relevant advice at the earliest possible moment. If you don't consider your future plans and strategise accordingly, you could end up with 200 people looking to you for leadership, and you have no idea how to even begin to manage them. So, in this case, if you're going to be managing your team yourself, you need to find a mentor who has done it before, who you can learn from, and who can help guide you until you're competent in that area.

Of course, you may receive different advice from different people – and that's fine. It's up to you to decide what's most relevant to you and your business. Even with great mentors to guide you, you *will* still have to make decisions. Advice, even when it's really good, isn't a mandate, and you'll need to decide what aligns and what doesn't.

A TALE OF TWO MENTORS

Generally, to be successful in business and life, you'll need to have two types of mentors or advisors around you. Type one mentors are people who can help you navigate the path that leads to your goals. They know exactly what you need to do in order to get where you want to go. You can tell them your objective, and they'll offer practical advice on how to reach it. You'll likely have a mixed bag of type one mentors, and many will come and go as required, depending on where you're at and what you need.

Type two mentors are people who you look up to – both on a business and personal level – and can point out the things you don't know you don't know. Generally, these people are long-term advisors who stick around for a while, although you may only call on them occasionally, often when you're totally stuck and don't know what to do next. You'll usually ask them questions like, "Have you done this before?" "Have you seen this before?" "What would *you* do?" If you can, it's better to engage with these people *before* you need them. Often, you'll tell them what you're doing, what you're trying to achieve, and they'll point out problems that wouldn't have been obvious to you until much later down the track.

So, type one mentors are ideal for addressing your immediate, strategic needs, while type two mentors are great at helping you navigate your long-term vision and identifying possible pitfalls before they arise.

When you bring experienced forward thinkers – type two mentors – into your mentorship group and inner circle, their knowledge, wisdom, and success rubs off on you. As Jim Rohn puts it, "You are the average of the five people you spend the most time with" – and the sentiment rings true. If you surround yourself with outstanding people, they're going to enhance you by association.

The beauty is, they don't even need to be people from within your industry. They don't need to have specific knowledge or a particular skill that's relevant to your business. You should already have a healthy pool of advisors who know your industry. However, some of the most creative solutions to your most difficult problems will come from people on the outside who can offer a fresh perspective. For example, someone from a different industry may deal with certain questions, issues, and decisions differently from someone in *your* industry. They may be able to offer unconventional advice that actually ends up being really relevant and effective.

It's the heart of entrepreneurship, right? We're not trying to do things in the typical way. Instead, we're searching for how we can do things differently – do them *better*. If that means seeking advice from unconventional sources, then that's what you need to do. A successful football coach or a violin teacher may use different techniques, frameworks, and tools compared to a tech entrepreneur, but a lot of what they do *will* translate to what *you're* doing, provided you don't botch the translation.

I truly believe that the mentors that will help get you to the highest levels of success are those who come from deep relationships. A fruitful mentorship is difficult to achieve if you don't have a genuine connection with someone. In business and in life, the meaningful relationships you build and nurture are some of your greatest assets.

1. Gain a sense of momentum from externals. Good mentors will turn you into a superhero.

2. Find little wins as fast as you can. Momentum builds on its success, like the saying, "Success builds success." Get it early and build on it.

3. Quickly identify if you're losing momentum. Look at leading indicators that help with this, and you won't be late to the party!

4. Build positive feedback loops. Each success should help catalyse further achievements.

5. Align opportunities with vision. Choose opportunities that reinforce and advance your core goals.

6. Sustain progress through challenges. Use the momentum of past successes to push through barriers.

7. Leverage small wins. Celebrate and build on smaller achievements to maintain motivation and momentum.

PHILOSOPHY
5

JUST DO SOMETHING - PROOF IN ACTION

IDEAS ARE CHEAP

One of the biggest things I see in the startup scene is people refusing to talk about their ideas because they think someone is going to steal them. The truth, however, is that ideas are cheap. I've got ideas. You've got ideas. The next person has some too. Good ideas aren't that hard to come by – it's good execution that's rare.

You could have an amazing, potentially world-changing idea but if you fail in your execution, or fail to even attempt to execute, your cheap idea – yes, even great ideas are cheap – will never be worth much. It won't become reality and reach its full potential. When you're in the execution phase, you start to realise that turning a concept into something tangible is a lot more difficult than simply saying, "Make it happen!" You're going to hit barriers you didn't know were there. You're going to have to work, struggle, and maybe even suffer. You might even start to question whether your game-changing idea is really as great as you think it is. But when you're building, creating, innovating, once the concept is sound and you've set a clear goal and know how you're going to get there, it's all about *doing*.

Sure, you could sit on a pile of great ideas, hoarding them and never mentioning them to anyone, but, at the end of the day, that's all you'll have: a pile of unrealised ideas. Let's be honest – some of them may not even be that great. But how will you know either way if you're not out there executing? Fundamentally, proof comes from action. You're much better off doing *something* and potentially failing than you are sitting around doing nothing. At worst, you learn some valuable lessons. Ideally, you successfully execute an idea and prove its greatness once and for all. Successful execution is what turns a cheap idea into a commodity, which *is* the goal, right?

In this chapter, in the spirit of driving you to *just do something,* we'll discuss the dos and don'ts of successfully executing an idea, my own experiences with proving a concept through action, the cultural differences between Silicon Valley and Australia, and why experience can sometimes be a liability rather than an asset. That last one may sound counterintuitive, but I swear it will make sense in the end.

HOT TIPS FOR A SUCCESSFUL EXECUTION

When preparing to execute an idea, you should always strategise and seek to understand exactly what the path to your ultimate goal looks like. In doing so, you'll quickly realise there's a reason why so many good ideas have never been undertaken. Smart people can talk themselves out of anything, and realising that taking an idea to the next stage demands some serious commitment and belief puts a lot of people off.

I've seen plenty of startups come up with amazing ideas but neglect to think beyond the concept itself and ask the necessary questions: "How do we create this thing?" "How do we finance it?" "How do we bring it to market?" "How do we attract the right customers?" "How do we scale?" "How do we make it cost-effective?" "How do we..." "How do we..." How do we..."

Ideally, you should be asking – and answering – these types of questions as soon as possible so you know what to expect during the execution phase. For example, if you're in the research and development space, you need to understand how you're going to recoup those initial costs over time. What's your rate of return going to be? If an idea isn't going to be feasible, you would want to know this as soon as possible – *before* you attempt to execute.

Investors certainly understand the importance of a smooth execution. They know that a failure to successfully execute is the biggest risk to their investment, and they'll want to know that you've considered everything before they hand over the big bucks. So, if you're creating a business, innovating, and going down the entrepreneurial path, de-risking the execution phase not only helps the business overall, but it also helps bring funding through the door. Whatever you can do to mitigate risk will literally pay off in the long run.

One of the best ways to improve your chances of success is to have an amazing team behind what you're doing. If you don't have the right people supporting your vision, the risk of a failed execution becomes very high. In most cases, you can't do everything, and you certainly can't *know* everything, so the key is to hire people who can fill those gaps. Even if you're a solo entre-preneur, you may need to enlist people to handle the technical side of things or another area where you lack expertise. If you're a part of a group of founders, hopefully each of you has different traits and skill sets that complement one another. For example, one person might know business; another might understand tech, and another might be an expert fundraiser. How you cover all the bases will depend on your situation. The important thing is that you *do* cover them.

At the core of any successful execution is a whole lot of tiny pieces that add up to one big outcome. It's not enough to do just one thing amazingly. To bring an idea to light and to life, you must consider every piece of the overall puzzle. Remember, at this stage of the process and beyond, your team is *everything*.

MY OWN EXECUTION

When we received a contract for a large order at Tiliter, we weren't ready for it, and I didn't know if we could make it happen. But it was an opportunity we couldn't refuse, so we accepted the challenge, and I aimed to do everything in my power to nail the execution. How do you achieve a near-impossible outcome? It all starts with a plan.

I mapped the journey from where we were to where we needed to go, with a clear timeline of events, and started us on our path. Of course, I implemented feedback loops for each important decision so we could assess our progress and make corrections along the way.

With a plan in place, which I followed to a tee, I was free to focus on the execution – but it wasn't all fun and games from there. The execution involved long days and countless hours of work. I had to organise subcontractors, shipping, supplies from overseas – everything we needed to make the plan a success – and, at the end of the day, I still had to deliver a profit. That part was important. You can move mountains to nail the perfect execution and achieve something amazing, but, ideally, you don't want to also achieve financial ruin in the process.

Naturally, I created a mental model that included everything that could possibly go wrong so I was ready for each hurdle along the way. For example, a supplier ran out of a key item we needed, but it was fine because I had three other suppliers lined up with negotiated prices already set – and it paid off. We fulfilled the contract, breathing a massive sigh of relief as we pulled off the near-impossible. At the same time, I set up a scalable process, with sustainability in mind, to set us up for the future, making the most out of the opportunity.

So, what's the key to a successful execution? Like I said, it all starts with a plan.

WE'RE A LONG WAY FROM SILICON VALLEY

When I first went to San Francisco in 2018, I quickly noticed the cultural differences between Silicon Valley and Australia. In Australia, we have more of a service-based economy, where many business owners are happy to just plod along, making a little bit of money as they go. If they're keeping the lights on and they're happy doing what they do, I can't argue that they're not successful, but serious ambition is rare. However, when I began immersing myself in the Silicon Valley startup scene, I noticed a major difference: they all wanted to achieve something really ambitious.

In recent years, the entrepreneurial ecosystem has evolved massively in Australia, but it still lags behind the US by a decade or more. When I visited Silicon Valley, I met founders who had felt the effects of tall poppy syndrome in the past, which is still a big problem in Australia. If someone grows too high, others want to cut them down and let them know they aren't all that. In the US, times have changed, and now success is mostly something to be celebrated.

Until we have a similar mindset shift in Australia, the key to overcoming tall poppy syndrome is surrounding yourself with people – founders, entrepreneurs, investors – who don't subscribe to that way of thinking. Instead, they provide an amazing support network that helps you grow.

I learnt that when other founders surrounded themselves with the right people, suddenly their confidence boomed, and so did their ability to execute. Instead of being cut down, they were being encouraged to reach for the stars, and it made a world of difference.

You know what they say: success breeds success. In the Silicon Valley startup scene, the networks, talent, learnings, and free flow of information combined to create a continuous cycle of success. For example, one company hired early employees from three unicorns, and *that* company went on to become a unicorn too. Those successful team members brought with them experience, confidence, investors, other employees, media – the list goes on.

When you fill your business with successful people, the risk associated with execution becomes so, so, *so* much lower. Essentially, the company becomes more attractive to the right candidates, more worthy of investment. On top of that, you're going to make better products because you've got talent, experience, and expertise behind you.

There is, however, a dark side to entrepreneurship and the pressure to succeed. I met a few founders who weren't doing so well, battling mental health issues that stemmed from failure or a fear of it. During my time in Silicon Valley, I saw so much material on suicide prevention and constant mentions of the high number of people who jump off the Golden Gate Bridge. All of this was a stark reminder of the pressures of entrepreneurship and the perils of failure, especially in a city filled with successful people. I talked to several founders who suffered from depression and some who even tried to take their own lives.

It was a grounding experience and a sharp reminder that we *all* need to keep a strong focus on our mental health, no matter where we are on our entrepreneurial journeys.

THE EXPERIENCE TRAP

With experience comes confidence and understanding – both great assets to have on an entrepreneurial journey. However, it is actually possible to have too much of a good thing.

Sometimes, experience makes us a little *too* confident and blinds us from seeing the best path forward. We may have done something a certain way in the past and achieved success, and we assume the same method will work every single time. But that's not how the world works. Sure, the same methods that brought you success in the past may work again for different ideas, but generally you're going to need to at least consider a fresh approach when executing a new concept.

Don't let experience make you cocky. You should approach every idea with a fresh perspective. Yes, considering past experiences is an important part of the process and if a previously successful method applies to the current situation, by all means, you should use it. For simple stuff especially, you can often apply the same processes again and again and get good results. However, when executing a complex idea, you need to consider all the options.

Successful entrepreneurs understand that their success isn't always repeatable using the exact same approach. Let your experience guide you, but don't let it blind you. If you do fall into the experience trap, you're likely to find yourself scratching your head, wondering why your tired and true method isn't working anymore. The entrepreneurial landscape is always shifting, and, if we want to stay in the game, we must shift with it.

KEY TAKEAWAYS FROM CHAPTER 5

JUST DO SOMETHING – PROOF IN ACTION

1. Don't get too caught up on an idea. People imagine great things all the time; the best go out and do it.

2. Own the responsibility of execution. At the end of the day, you can't control everything, but you sure can have a plan for the most likely scenarios. Don't ignore them and blindly do something. Instead, make sure you calculate your efforts.

3. Action leads to insight. Practical experience often teaches more than theoretical planning.

4. Use iterative development. Launch small, learn fast, and iterate based on real feedback.

5. Overcome fear of failure. Accept that mistakes are part of the learning process.

6. Proof lies in execution. Demonstrating capability through action builds credibility and confidence.

PHILOSOPHY

6

SELL THE FUTURE OR FAIL

THE FASTER HORSES MENTALITY

As entrepreneurs, we can't just focus on shaping the future through innovation; we also have to *sell* the future. The problem is that people often don't know what they want until it's right there, staring them in the face. There's a quote that some attribute to Henry Ford, although the actual origin is a little murky, that sums up the situation nicely: "If I had asked people what they wanted, they would have said faster horses." Whether Ford actually said the quote or not doesn't matter. Either way, the statement highlights one of the biggest struggles of an entrepreneur: convincing people that your innovative new product is the solution to their problem; that is, *selling the future.*

I'm not saying that faster, stronger, more tireless horses wouldn't have been great at the time, but they wouldn't have had the massive impact that the automobile did. As entrepreneurs, we're generally looking beyond the lacklustre goal of 'slightly better' to the exciting realm of groundbreaking, game-changing, *world-shattering.* Seeing the future is one thing; selling it is a whole other game. It's one that can be really difficult to win, especially if you're trying to push the boundaries.

So, how confident are you about selling the future? If you do lack confidence in this area, let's aim to change that now. In this chapter, we'll discuss the pitfall of innovating for the sake of innovation, seeing the future, selling the future, and the importance of giving value to your customers.

INNOVATION FOR THE SAKE OF INNOVATION

Over the years, I've seen a lot of people overcomplicate simple things in the pursuit of innovation. It's innovation for innovation's sake, which, quite frankly, is a waste of time and resources. When creating a new product, some entrepreneurs wrongly focus on the product itself, starting with the question: "What can we create?" Really, the question should be: "What problem can we solve?"

When it comes to selling a product, people with minimal sales experience typically focus on spruiking the features rather than framing their offer as the solution to someone's problem. Naturally, when we create technology simply for the sake of creating something, selling the product as a solution is difficult. Therefore, ideally you should be thinking about the problem well before you begin to conceptualise a product.

If you're too focused on innovating over problem-solving, you could end up creating an overcomplicated product when a more straightforward approach would have sufficed. When you solve a complex problem with a seemingly simple solution, you catch people's attention. That's right – keeping it simple is a great way to wow your audience. How do you ensure simplicity when it's warranted? Well, there's one way you can pretty much guarantee it. When you develop a product with a specific problem in mind, naturally, you should arrive at the simplest solution. You're still innovative; you're just doing it in a way that actually makes sense and, importantly, that investors and customers can understand.

Let's take Linktree, for example. Essentially, the product solves the problem of not being able to easily share multiple links without creating an entire website. How does it solve this issue? By displaying all of your chosen links on one shareable page. Suddenly, you're able to share your social media profiles, a calendar link, a blog, and more without having to finance, build, and maintain a website. The brains behind Linktree didn't necessarily need to create any new technology or innovate in a big way; they just had to arrive at a solution that made sense. Only a product that was created with a problem in mind could be so simple yet effective.

So, if you're solving a problem, you should be doing it in the quickest, simplest, and most effective way possible. When you take this approach, you'll often find that you naturally start to innovate more and more along the way. Innovation for the sake of innovation doesn't create good products. Solving problems should always be your goal. Like many things in life, innovation is best when it happens naturally. It shouldn't be something you try to force.

EVERY ENTREPRENEUR NEEDS A CRYSTAL BALL

Before you sell the future, you need to know what the future looks like so you can understand what people need before *they* know they need it. Remember, most people refuse to imagine anything beyond better versions of the things they already have, as highlighted in the 'faster horses' example. It's up to you to stretch *your* imagination and consider what's truly possible, even if those possibilities seem a little outrageous – or totally insane – at first.

When identifying the problem you want to solve, looking into the future is a critical part of the process. What does the future look like? How will technology have progressed? How will culture have shifted? It's important to consider as many variables as possible. Yes, that includes the cultural landscape and available infrastructure. Basically, you want to get a vision of the future that's as clear as possible so you know which problems will be relevant and what resources will be available to fuel the solution. You may identify a problem that you can't easily solve with today's tech. Perhaps the ideal solution requires more efficient battery technology, faster internet, or something else before it becomes viable. That's why thinking into the future is so important. It allows you to see solutions that others don't even know are possible – because they're not. Yet.

If you want to get a good glimpse of the future, you should pay attention to what the more advanced countries are doing. What are they focusing on? What infrastructure are they developing? What research and development are they pushing? Once upon a time, creating a product that relied on constant cellular reception wouldn't have been viable. However, if you examined where technology was headed – cellular towers everywhere! – you could have begun developing your product early and had the groundwork in place ready for the future, placing yourself well in front of any competition.

So, what does the future look like? Does it involve interplanetary space travel? Quantum computers? Fusion energy? With the way-too-wealthy investing so much money into rockets, interplanetary space travel certainly seems like a possibility. If so, we could be in for some exciting times. With that said, forecasting the future isn't only about the fun stuff. You should also take the time to talk to governments and understand where they're putting their money. What's *their* vision of the future? Because when the future does arrive, much of it will be shaped by government policy.

So, the trick to forming a clear picture of the future is to analyse as many facets of society as possible: technology, culture, infrastructure, research and development, government, and so on. Once you pull everything together, you should have enough information to determine the problem you're going to solve and start creating a plan for how you're going to solve it. Remember, execution is everything, and it's where most entrepreneurs hit their biggest barriers.

The world needs people who have a vision. We need people who say, "I want the world to be like *this*, and I believe we can make it happen." We need people who are willing to do whatever it takes to make that vision a reality, which could involve creating a product or even investing in someone else's creation. We need people who are not just capable of imagining the future but are also eager to shape it.

SOME PEOPLE THOUGHT THE INTERNET WOULD NEVER CATCH ON

Once you have identified the problem you want to solve, have a clear vision of the future, and you've created a roadmap to get you there, you're ready to start selling that future. How do you successfully do this? Honestly, a lot of trial and error. At the start of your entrepreneurial journey, your primary fuel source will likely be the belief that your idea *is* the future. You'll be determined to prove it to yourself and the world. If your idea seems even slightly crazy, people will doubt you. It's expected and all a part of the process. But if you genuinely believe in what you're creating, you'll naturally start to win people over.

With that said, you can't sell the future based solely on an unshakable belief. If you want to increase your reach and influence, establishing strong partnerships and relationships with the right people is crucial. When you're selling the future, especially when there's no solid science behind what you're proposing and you're operating on pure belief, the support of others can go a long way. You will, of course, need to find people who also believe in your vision, so selling the future starts here.

When you're selling your vision, it's not only important to sell *what* you're doing but also *how* you're going to do it. Often, the 'what' makes a lot of sense. For example, you could say we need to create flying cars to address congestion on our roads. The solution is a little on the crazy side, but the overall idea makes sense. Congestion *is* a problem, and flying cars could be a way to solve it. But could you actually execute that idea? Are flying cars the quickest, simplest, most effective solution? Can you sell this vision of the future to the people who matter?

When selling the future, your aim is to win people over. You want them to believe in your vision as much as you do. As entrepreneurs, we're often impatient for change. We know what the future looks like, and we want it *now*. However, selling the future is rarely an overnight process. In truth, it's a series of small wins that eventually add up to a greater outcome: people buying in to your vision. There's only so much you can do in the short-term to win people over. However, as you begin to prove your concept through action, you'll convert more people. We've seen the same process play out with emerging technology in the past.

Think about where the concept of autonomous cars began. In the early 2000s, the path to self-driving vehicles started with lane assist, a system that warns drivers when they're leaving their lane without indicating. The technology was created to address the problem of distraction and driver fatigue. Back when lane assist first appeared on the market, the idea of fully autonomous vehicles must have seemed completely insane. As well as being great tech, lane assist was a necessary step towards a future in which cars really do drive themselves. The technology to make it happen wasn't there in the beginning, but the belief that it eventually would be certainly existed in the minds of some visionaries. By nature, most people resist drastic change. Therefore, the key to getting them to buy in to your vision of the future is to take them there one small step at a time. As much as your entrepreneurial spirit might protest, you can't rush these things. Eventually, if your execution is sound, people will flip to your way of thinking.

Frequently, we see concepts that were once considered science fiction come into being. Aeroplanes. Space travel. *The internet*. Imagine trying to sell the idea of the internet to someone in the early 1900s before computer networking was even invented. "All of the information that exists in the world will be accessible anytime, anywhere via a global network called the internet." It would be a tough sell; that's for sure. Even as late as the mid-90s, as the internet was becoming more mainstream, the technology still had its doubters.

In a 1995 *Newsweek* article, astronomer Clifford Stoll wrote, "Do our computer pundits lack all common sense? The truth in [sic] no online database will replace your daily newspaper, no CD-ROM can take the place of a competent teacher and no computer network will change the way government works."[3] He goes on to reject the idea that we would ever buy books over the internet – what a crazy concept! The rapid growth of Amazon, which Jeff Bezos had already established when the article was published, must have come as a shock. Now, Stoll wasn't a stupid guy. He was a respected scientist, teacher, and author. He also wasn't unfamiliar with the internet, claiming to have spent two decades online before he wrote the article, and this was in *1995* – he was practically a pioneer of the technology. It's likely that Clifford Stoll understood more about the internet than almost anyone on Earth. So, why were his predictions so far from reality? Because no one had successfully sold him the future. It's not that he thought online shopping, news access, and educational games weren't possible, but he couldn't imagine a world where people would want these things. At his core, Stoll was a scientist, not an entrepreneur, and it would take visionaries like Jeff Bezos and eBay founder Pierre Omidyar to sell the future to the masses and prove him wrong.

For the record, in 2010, Stoll acknowledged his mistake: "Wrong? Yep."[4]

THE VALUE OF ADDING VALUE

When you're conceptualising and creating a product, it's important to be customer-centric. That doesn't mean putting the customer first but putting *the value* to the customer first. People always think they know what they want, but, as an entrepreneur, which is basically an expert in knowing what people *really* want, you're already seeing past their misguided demands. You're adding value by giving them the thing they didn't know they needed. If, however, you give in to customer demands instead of selling the future, you're taking the easy way out. On top of that, you're probably not adding a lot of value to your product or your business.

You don't even need to have the most refined, polished product on the market if you're giving your customers awesome value. For instance, a lot of people will put up with a glitchy app if it has all the functions and features they need. Maybe it's a fitness app that tracks all the metrics they want tracked, but the interface is a little clunky, and the app occasionally freezes and needs to be restarted. Of course, customers would prefer the product to work perfectly every time, but maybe it's free to use, which would appeal to a certain consumer. Sure, a more expensive app might offer the same features without the annoying glitches, but a paid product would be aimed at a different type of buyer. The key is to know your market and understand how to best solve their problem.

Once you've got people on board and they're using your product, gathering feedback is important. You need to understand the customer experience thoroughly and as completely as possible. In the case of the app example, you would likely receive a lot of negative feedback about the clunkiness of the software, which you would take on board. Then you would work towards fixing those issues when it's feasible to do so. But you knew your market from the beginning, and you understood that your customers would be willing to put up with a few bugs if the features were there and the price was right.

Personally, I'm a big fan of getting as much feedback as possible. You should, of course, always make your own decisions, but at least they will be informed decisions. As an entrepreneur, it's critical that you don't try to action every piece of feedback you receive. Yes, you should try to understand what people are saying and where they're coming from, but *you* must choose the path you take. Don't let others steer you in a direction that leads away from your defined goals.

KEY TAKEAWAYS FROM CHAPTER 6

SELL THE FUTURE OR FAIL

1. Bet on what the future looks like and shape what you're doing on that.

2. Adding value is the start of any product or service. There's no sense working on something because it seems 'cool' or because maybe you 'think' someone might want it. Instead, go out and learn if people actually want what you want to create. Listen to what they want, ask the right questions, and ensure you analyse their responses based on where you see the future going.

3. Vision drives investment. A clear and compelling vision can attract investment and customer interest.

4. Develop a future-oriented strategy. Develop strategies that not only address current needs but also anticipate future market trends.

5. Communicate potential impact. Clearly articulate the potential impact of your vision to stakeholders.

6. Innovate with purpose. Innovation should aim to solve future problems, not just current ones.

PHILOSOPHY

7

TAKE EVERYTHING SERIOUSLY, BUT DON'T TAKE EVERYTHING TOO SERIOUSLY

IT'S NOTHING PERSONAL

You won't get far in business if you don't take what you're doing seriously. To be successful, you must be willing to put in the effort. If you're too casual in your approach, you're going to be overshadowed by those who are more serious. With that said, taking things *too* seriously can be just as detrimental.

When you're running a business, if you want to stay sane, you must disconnect your identity from the business itself. You can't take everything personally. Some of the most challenging times for me as an entrepreneur were when I thought my identity was the business. I was not only taking everything seriously, but I was also taking it personally. Every loss, whether it was a minor hiccup or a major failure, hit hard. When you let everything get to you like that, you risk getting stuck in a downward spiral, constantly overthinking every decision and unfavourable outcome.

However, when I was able to grow on a personal level and separate my identity from the business, life became much more manageable – even enjoyable – and success came easier. Interestingly, as I grew personally, the personality and vibe of the business reflected that change, growing with me. When you stop taking everything personally, you're better able to remove emotion from your decisions, which means the choices you make come from a more rational place. We want to be making the best decisions possible, right?

Whether in life or business, taking something too seriously is a great way to suck all the fun out of it. As entrepreneurs, we can get so focused on our destination and the pitfalls and potholes along the way that we forget to enjoy the ride. Wouldn't it be nice if you could achieve success *and* have fun doing it? It's not a pipedream. Fundamentally, achieving a healthy balance of taking everything seriously but not too seriously is all a matter of mindset, which is something you absolutely can control. During your entrepreneurial journey, you're going to face countless struggles. You're going to be tested in many different ways. In this chapter, we'll discuss the ugly truth of entrepreneurship, learning to roll with the punches, why a lot of entrepreneurs are arseholes – it's true! – and how to separate the critics from the haters.

YOU'LL HAVE 99 PROBLEMS

From the outside, entrepreneurship can look like a glamorous undertaking, especially when we only pay attention to the success stories. But is it as glamorous as it looks? The short answer – no.

In the beginning, you probably won't have a lot to lose. Perhaps you've had a genius idea that's just a little crazy or a crazy idea that's just a little genius, and you're ready to put the concept to the test. At any point in your journey, the risks are always the same, but the consequences grow with success. While there's definitely a lot of pressure at the start, that pressure and the stress that accompanies it only increases as the business grows. For example, if a side hustle fails, you'll likely just try something else. However, as you get further down the line, the consequences of going bust become much larger. You might owe investors money; you might have outstandings you need to pay; you might be failing your customers. On a personal level, you may be supporting a family and have a mortgage to pay. Once you reach a certain point in your journey, the consequences of failure become astronomical, adding to the pressure and stress you might be feeling. I'm telling you this so you know exactly what you're getting yourself into should you choose the path of an entrepreneur. It's not all glitz and glamour; that's a fact.

The 'higher consequences' principle applies to other careers too. For instance, if you're an elite athlete, standards are higher, and room for error is much smaller, especially at the highest level. If you do something wrong, everyone's going to know about it, and, depending on the situation, the consequences could be significant. You could cost yourself or your team an important win. You could lose a big sponsorship. If you fuck up epically enough, you could lose your whole career. On the flip side, if you're playing division five of a local competition, you're not going to face nearly as much scrutiny. The stakes just aren't as high. Sure, if you mess up majorly during a game, your coach might have a few choice words to say on the matter, but you'll likely just have a beer afterwards and shrug it off.

If you're under the impression that success and growth are the solutions to all the problems startups face early on, I've got some unfortunate news for you: your problems don't change. It's just the stakes that change. I frequently see entrepreneurs who think getting to that next step will make all of their problems disappear. But what really happens is they reach that step and not only are the problems still there, but they're a whole lot bigger. If a decision doesn't pay off and you take a hit financially, instead of losing a bit of money, you could lose a lot. When you're scaling, instead of scaling with a couple of people, you could be scaling with over 100. As the business grows, the stakes get higher – it's inevitable – and stress can increase if you're taking things too seriously.

It may sound like I'm implying that the life of an entrepreneur is all stress and struggle. While much of it is, you can still have fun with it. And if you play the game right, you can eventually remove founder dependency, which means you can limit or redefine your role in the company as you see fit. For many entrepreneurs, that's the aim: to create an organisation that's bigger than any one person. When you do finally reach that point, it feels like the world is being lifted off your shoulders. Who's doing the lifting? That would be the awesome team you've assembled. So, while the problems of the business won't go away, they don't have to be solely *your* problems. See, it does get better. However, until you reach a point where you have teams working on all of your problems, big and small, as the founder, you're going to be taking the brunt of every blow.

With that said, not everyone finds the idea of stepping back and letting others handle certain aspects of the business calming. In fact, it can stress some people out even more. Some entrepreneurs feel like they have to be fully in control – they must be the sole decision-maker. On the flip side, many others are happy to empower their teams to make decisions and get things done. Neither approach is fundamentally right or wrong. However, you need to ask yourself: Can you really do *everything* yourself? As your business grows, the answer to that question will likely become a resounding 'no'.

All right, it's time for some good news. As an entrepreneur, if you're building wealth along the way, the journey does get easier. When you don't have to worry about money, you have a lot more freedom and, if you choose, life can get a bit more glamorous. However, the reality is that wealth is a by-product of entrepreneurship. In my experience, entrepreneurs who put wealth before the product ultimately fail. To be successful, your focus should be on creating something that solves a problem and people are eager to adopt. If you can do this, wealth will naturally flow from there.

I talk to so many people who see the lifestyles of successful entrepreneurs, and they want the same for themselves *without* doing all the hard work to get there. Essentially, they want to arrive at the finish line and receive their medal without running the race. How far do you think these people get in business? Sure, they may start down the entrepreneurial path but when they hit the hard stages, the rough terrain, they give up because it's not all the glitz and glamour they imagined. In fact, it's a far cry from the glamorous lives their idles present on social media. The reality is, it takes so much hard work to become super successful. Funnily enough, when you get there, you may not even realise you've 'made it'. Sometimes it takes someone else to point it out.

In the meantime, don't look at all the glitz on social media and assume that's what you'll automatically achieve. It doesn't work like that. It may not even be the lifestyle that's right for you. Either way, if you want to be truly successful, put in the work, take the blows, and earn your spot at the top.

GETTING SERIOUS ABOUT NOT TAKING THINGS TOO SERIOUSLY

I know that "don't take things too seriously" is easier said than done. When the pressure and stress levels increase, reacting with good humour isn't easy. You're probably not going to become a stoic overnight. The key to not taking things too seriously is to build habits and find methods that help you deal with the stress.

Whenever I'm hiring, I always ask candidates, "Do you have a personal method for dealing with stress?" It's an interesting question because the answers vary so widely. Some responses I get are fairly unsurprising: meditation, nature walks, calming music. However, some people give answers that seem counterintuitive, such as, "I just work harder." On the surface, it might seem like these people are just trying to give a good interview response, but, in most cases, it genuinely is how these people operate.

My point is that there are so many different ways people deal with stress, so you need to find a method that works for you and build habits around that solution. If meditating for 20 minutes in the morning is your remedy, make it a habit. Don't neglect the self-care you need to get through the day, week, month, year, and beyond. For most people, working harder isn't the solution. Many of us need to disconnect from our work environments in order to recharge. We need to switch off after a certain hour, spend time with our families, or just touch grass every now and then.

Fitness is a great outlet for many of us. Staying fit, healthy, and active is important for anyone who wants to effectively navigate the stresses of business and life. Pick a sport or a flavour of exercise you enjoy and build a healthy habit around it. When you're pushing yourself physically, focusing on negative thoughts becomes difficult. If you are in a negative mental spiral, performing some intense or focused exercise is a great way to escape it.

In the past, when I didn't find outlets for my stress, I experienced some of the worst times in business and in my personal life too. When you're taking everything too seriously, it's difficult to recognise the wins, which means you're only focusing on the losses. That type of mindset becomes a black hole that pulls you in, further and further, sucking all the positivity out of the air. Once you're too far in, escape feels impossible. You may think that working harder will solve the problem when what you really need is a weekend off. I once heard someone say that a good measure of how good someone is at their job is how often they're able to play golf. The reality is that if you have time to golf regularly – or do whatever recreational activity you enjoy – you're probably doing better than the person who doesn't have the time. Working hard is important; however, taking time to unwind and enjoy life is not only necessary for stress relief, but it's also a sign of success.

REJECTION? GET USED TO IT

As an entrepreneur, you're going to face rejection after rejection after rejection after – you get the point. Investors will turn you down, and potential customers will refuse to use your product. But that's okay. In fact, it's expected in the beginning. The aim isn't to avoid rejection. Instead, you should learn how to handle it well.

When you've been rejected countless times, you may be tempted to change your product to meet other people's needs, demands, or expectations. Don't do this. You need to be confident in what you're selling and have absolute belief in your vision. It goes back to the idea of selling the future. If your idea is sound in *your* mind, then you should be backing it all the way, even if others reject it. Sure, your execution may change, but the concept and product itself should largely remain the same. If you keep moving the goalposts, you'll end up creating something that doesn't align with your vision and may not even be what people actually need. Instead of selling the future, you could end up with faster horses.

Investors will be some of your harshest critics, which is totally fair. If they invest a significant amount of money in your product, they have a lot more to lose than, say, the average customer. They may be taking a substantial risk, and anyone with the means to invest in a startup is likely at least somewhat rational with their investments.

Personally, I've been rejected by hundreds of investors, but I kept putting myself and the product out there – because it only takes one person to say yes. When it comes to investors, there are different types with different outlooks, and they're all looking for different things. I've seen businesses that never get past the investment stage because they keep changing their products to match what they think investors want. They change what they're presenting based on who they're presenting to, and what the actual product is gets muddled. They start to question their vision and what they're offering, and confidence plummets.

When you're facing rejection after rejection from investors, you have to be stubborn and a little cocksure. *I'm not wrong – it's everyone else who's wrong!* Eventually, if you've got an awesome product and can successfully sell the future to the right person, you will secure funding.

As mentioned, the other big source of rejection is customers. You need early adopters to use your product, but building trust in the beginning can be difficult. Occasionally, something goes viral and undergoes rapid adoption, but, for the most part, you need to build trust with potential clients before they'll accept you and your product, especially in the B2B (business-to-business) space.

During the early days of one of my startups, when we were trying to sell our AI-powered produce-recognition technology, we faced a lot of rejection. At one point, the executives at an extremely large company practically laughed us out of the room – and they were right to do so. The technology we were presenting was amateur at the time, and clearly we had failed to sell the future we envisioned and would eventually achieve. Two years later, that company became one of our biggest customers.

Just because you get a 'no' now, it doesn't mean you won't eventually get a 'yes'. If we had taken that initial rejection seriously, and personally, we likely wouldn't have tried again later down the track. We might have given up on the whole idea right there and then. They didn't just close the door – they practically slammed it in our faces. Fortunately, we were stubborn, and we didn't change the direction of the business or stray from our initial vision. We just kept pushing forward until we got the magic 'yes'.

WHY ARE SO MANY ENTREPRENEURS ARSEHOLES?

This might sound bad, but you'll do better in the business world if you can numb your emotions. I'm not saying you should become an emotionless robot, but making decisions fuelled by emotion, especially after a big rejection, is a fast path to failure.

Early in my career, I attended a lot of seminars, where I met some amazing entrepreneurs, but I kept asking myself one question: *Why are they all such arseholes?* Now, not every successful entrepreneur is in fact an arsehole, but I did notice a trend.

Once I reached a certain point in my journey, I found my answer. As an entrepreneur, you're going to have to deal with constant doubt, rejection, and an endless supply of problems. If you don't learn how to numb yourself to all of it, you're going to become an emotional wreck. In business, decisions based solely on emotion rarely pay off. Unstable emotions lead to an unstable business. If you're emotionally reacting to every bit of input you receive, you may end up going in a direction that's at odds with your initial vision and, ultimately, doesn't lead to success.

I'm not saying you have to become an arsehole to succeed – not at all – but you do have to be rational in your thinking and your actions. With that said, as you gain success and your expectations of yourself grow, your expectations of others will likely grow too. You expect the best from people, which, if you don't channel this expectation well, could turn you into an arsehole in the eyes of those around you.

There's a fine line between numbing your emotions and becoming the arsehole. I definitely went through a phase where I crossed that line and headed into arsehole territory. My expectations of others were so high that I would get upset whenever someone wasn't performing. For example, if I was at a restaurant and my meal took too long to arrive, I would create an uncomfortable situation that usually involved some rudeness and ended with me asking for my money back.

Eventually, I became aware of what I was doing and made some changes. I know how easy it is to fall into that type of behaviour, but acting like an arsehole doesn't benefit you or anyone else in the long run. Once you're aware of what you're doing, self-management is key. You can find better ways to react to negative situations without getting emotional and without alienating those around you. Now when someone brings me bad news, I respond with "good." It's a somewhat sarcastic response, but it injects some positivity into the situation. As we know, most failures are just a step towards success, so why act otherwise?

MAYBE (A CHINESE PROVERB)

Have you heard the Chinese proverb about the man and the horses? Regardless, I'm going to tell it now. So, there's a man in a village who has a horse he relies on every day. Practically his whole life revolves around this horse. He needs it to plough the fields, to ride on hunts, and for transportation. Without it, he and his family would likely starve.

One day, the horse runs away, and a group of villagers comes to console the man. "This is terrible," they say.

"Maybe," the man says and, to the confusion of the villagers, leaves it at that.

The next day, the horse returns, but nine wild horses have come with it, which the man claims as his own.

Once again, a group of villagers comes to see him. "This is a blessing," they say.

"Maybe," the man says again.

The next day, the man's son is riding one of the wild horses, attempting to tame it. However, the animal bucks him, and the boy falls and breaks his leg.

Naturally, a group of villagers comes to investigate. "What a terrible accident," they say.

"Maybe," the man says.

By coincidence, the very next day, the military begins conscripting people for war. The man's son is eligible but when the recruiters examine the boy's broken leg, they announce that he's exempt. He's no good to the military in his current condition.

Of course, a group from the village comes to see the man – how could they resist? "Your son doesn't have to go to war. That's great news," they say.

The man smiles. "Maybe."

When you face challenges or even total disasters in business, remember that those problems are only as big as you choose to make them. Really, they only have the gravity you assign them.

When someone approaches you to deliver the news that you've lost your metaphorical horse – and this *will* happen at some point

– how will you react? Will you let it derail your mood, your day, your business? Or will you simply respond with "good" and keep moving forward?

CONSTRUCTIVE CRITICISM VS. DESTRUCTIVE HATE

If you're creating something truly innovative, you're going to encounter a lot of doubters. People will question what you're doing, and some will think you've lost your mind. But that's fine. In fact, it might be a sign that you're on the right track. No one outside of the business is likely to understand what's happening internally, and they're certainly not going to know what's happening inside your mind. Although, who knows? Mind-reading technology could very well be around the corner. Regardless, whether criticism is valid or not comes down to your own assessment.

But there's a catch: that assessment can be very hard to make. As you progress, you're going to meet some really amazing, successful people who are actually quite spiteful. They might be jealous; they might not get what you're doing, or they might have a completely different outlook on life. Either way, identifying whose advice you can trust is critical. Where is their criticism coming from? Is it from a positive place? Or do they have ulterior motives? Understanding who you can trust should be your number one priority when it comes to taking criticism. Now, I'm not saying you should accept every piece of criticism a trusted source flings your way, but knowing who has your best interests at heart helps filter out a lot of the noise – that is, the worthless doubt and baseless hate.

When I didn't want to deal with unsolicited, unconstructive criticism, I would do my best to avoid those types of conversations. After a while, being able to tell who's itching to throw some negativity your way gets fairly easy. You learn to recognise these people straight away. To avoid the conversation, I would just tell people I was a postie or something else uncontroversial. So, if you want to avoid unconstructive criticism, reading the room is key – and always have a fake job title ready to shut down any interrogation.

Honestly, unless you enjoy fighting those battles, they're a waste of time and effort. If you do find yourself fighting every pointless fight, you may need to ask yourself, *Am I taking this too seriously?* You're never going to win everyone over – it's just not possible. You're going to upset a few people along the way, but it's a necessary part of the journey. It may sound cliché but once you accept that you can't make everyone happy, you'll become much happier yourself.

Whenever you receive constructive criticism, you should weigh it against the truth of and intent behind what you're doing. Is the criticism still valid? It's okay to reject advice from a trusted source if that advice misaligns with your goals. A lot of entrepreneurs spend countless hours educating themselves, reading books — like this one – attending seminars, continuously searching for 'the answer'. But there is no answer, no secret to success. More accurately, there are *infinite* answers, and the one that solves someone else's problem may not solve yours. Ultimately, only you can decide if advice or criticism is worth accepting. However, the only way to know for sure whether you've got the right answer is to act on it and see what happens.

KEY TAKEAWAYS FROM CHAPTER 7

1. There are going to be critics – one of them could even be you. You need to find a way to manage them. To an extent, they could even be right. Be open, be kind, be willing to not take things too personally.

2. Rejection is a part of life. No matter what, you will face rejection at some point in your personal life, and business is no different. Learn from it but also stay true to yourself and your beliefs.

3. Don't be an arsehole – it helps nobody. As hard as it gets, you need to manage your emotions.

4. Balance is key. Maintain professionalism without losing the ability to enjoy the journey.

5. Find resilience in humour. Use humour as a tool to cope with setbacks and maintain team morale.

6. Get serious about commitments. Honour your commitments and take your responsibilities seriously.

7. Have flexibility in perspective. Allow room for lightheartedness, which can foster a positive work environment and encourage creative thinking.

PHILOSOPHY

8

BUSINESS CAN BE SHORT, BUT SO CAN LIFE – SEIZE OPPORTUNITY

RISKY BUSINESS

As an entrepreneur, if you're not taking risks, you're probably not innovating. You're probably not moving the dial. You're probably on the short road to stagnation.

I'm not saying you should be out there constantly risking it all on a whim. However, the businesses that seize opportunity and push themselves to evolve are our future success stories.

You could be forgiven for thinking that business is meant to be risky. At least, we expect it to come with its fair share of risks. If founding a startup were a sure path to success, everyone would be doing it *and* succeeding. At times, you will need to gamble on an outcome. With that said, there are plenty of ways to recognise the risks, know exactly what you're getting yourself into, and prepare for the worst should a bet not pay off.

In this chapter, we'll discuss how to mitigate risk in every decision you make, what happens when brands play it too safe and refuse to evolve (spoiler – it doesn't end well), and what I learnt from a near-death experience. To tie it all off, we'll also discuss the importance of celebrating our wins.

As they say, you've got to risk it for the biscuit – or for the brisket, if meat is more your thing. Either way, opportunity isn't going to seize itself. If you want to succeed, you've got to take action.

TAKING THE RISK OUT OF RISK-TAKING

To avoid taking unnecessary risks, you need to learn to predict the future. Simple, right? When you use the right mental models, you can understand what will happen ahead of time. The more you know, the better you can prepare for the worst.

Whenever I'm taking a risk, I perform a premortem. I analyse what could go wrong, how it could go wrong, and what the outcomes might be. Once you understand what *could* go wrong, you're in a better position to stop it from happening. Through this process, you may even decide the risk isn't worth the potential consequences of failure. In those cases, it's best to consider an alternative approach.

But when you utilise your mental models and gain a deeper understanding of the risks, you're able to navigate the landscape more confidently and, hopefully, steer yourself to success.

Another big part of avoiding unnecessary failure is knowing what you do well. Rather than trying to do a lot of things adequately, you should focus on doing what you do well – and do it *really* well. There's no room for mediocrity in the startup scene. If a certain path isn't going to facilitate your best work, you may need to rethink the route you're taking. There's no point performing at an okay level. Instead, you should find what you excel at and run with it. What are your strengths? Play to them. By focusing on doing what you do well, you're actually removing a lot of the risk right at the beginning.

Let's face it – without a certain amount of risk-taking, whether you're in business, on the footy field, or just living life, the rewards aren't going to be as high. If you want a good serving of the brisket, you know what you need to do.

INNOVATE, OR STAGNATE

If you fail to innovate, you will stagnate. You could have the best product, service, business on the block but if you stop evolving once you reach success, that success won't last.

I've seen it time and time again: successful companies that start neglecting innovation, research and development funding, *vision*. Before they know it, competitors are coming out of the woodwork to snatch their market from them. This is why so many startups end up beating established businesses. They're willing to take more risks; therefore, they can move much faster than competitors, who are stuck playing it safe.

In the beginning, you generally have little to lose. Sure, you might have invested your life savings in the business and perhaps quit your day job, but the stakes aren't super high. However, once you start converting customers and bringing on investors, shareholders, and other stakeholders, suddenly you've got a *lot* to lose if you make a bad decision or take a massive risk that doesn't pay off.

With that said, the ability to take risks and weather the potential fallout of failure works on a bell curve. Like I said, at the start, you don't have much to lose, not in the grand scheme of things, anyway. But once your business reaches a certain level of success, there's too much at stake to take those big risks that got you there in the first place. If, however, you can survive that stage with your market and reputation intact, suddenly you're in a better position to start taking risks again. At a certain point, you practically become too big to fail. I say 'practically' because, let's face it, any business can fail. But once you reach a certain level, you would almost have to actively be trying to fail to tank the business. You would have to make a series of insanely bad decisions and take a number of careless risks.

When a great company is sitting near the top of the bell curve, typically they will do a bunch of acquisitions. That way, they gain innovation, improve their products, and continue to grow without taking on the risk of innovation internally. They don't need to sink time, money, and other resources into ideas that may or may not succeed. Instead, they can find something that's already working quite well and fits the business, and import that innovation relatively risk-free. Sure, a company with a product, idea, or technology that's already showing promise isn't cheap to acquire, but you're not just buying what they have. You're also buying time. By bypassing the time constraint of research and development, you're effectively getting your product to market quicker. And timing is everything, right? On top of that, if you make a good acquisition, you might be able to nab a company for less than the cost of internal research and development – an ideal outcome.

When we talk about startups and entrepreneurship, we're generally referring to private companies, but they aren't the entire picture. To understand the complete picture, we should also consider public companies. When the public markets are down, adding value to your stock is difficult. Typically, acquiring other companies is a good way to boost that value. So, for a public company, it's not just about avoiding stagnation from an innovation perspective but also from a share price standpoint. Needless to say, shareholder return is important, and it could either be a driving force for innovation or one that ultimately steers you in the wrong direction. Sacrificing long-term success for short-term profit can be a death sentence for some companies.

Again, continued growth and success come down to focusing on what you do really well. As your business reaches a certain level, you'll arrive at a point where you'll need to decide what to double down on. What do I mean by this? You'll need to decide what product, feature, service, idea – whatever it is – you do best and, importantly, makes sense to keep doing. If you double down on the *wrong* aspect of your business, well, there are plenty of real-world examples that demonstrate what this looks like.

Let's take BlackBerry, for example. It doubled down on the idea that keyboards would continue to be a dominant feature of modern smartphones, and touchscreens wouldn't be relevant within the space. *Big* whoops. They made a risky gamble and essentially watched their market share melt away over several years due to the heat of the iPhone and Android-powered devices. In contrast, Apple doubled down on touchscreen technology and the idea that third-party apps would play a critical role in future mobile devices. As we know, their bet paid off. So, while it's important to focus on what you do best – like smartphone keyboards, for example – it's equally as, if not more, important to ensure that thing has a future.

Almost every move you make in business comes with risks. The key is understanding those risks and making the best possible decision based on the information you have. While we can't predict the future perfectly, we can make some pretty good guesses. If you're not looking ahead, if you're not innovating and evolving with the times, you risk becoming another casualty in the fight to stay relevant. Even the giants – those businesses at the top of their industries – can fall. It has happened before, and it will happen again. History is an excellent teacher.

WHEN GIANTS FALL (A CAUTIONARY TALE)

What ever happened to the Sony Walkman, which dominated the portable music space for decades? Why is Nokia no longer a go-to mobile phone brand? Why aren't kids demanding an Atari under the Christmas tree anymore? At one point, Sony (Walkman), Nokia, and Atari dominated their respective industries, but now they're little more than an afterthought to most people.

So, what went wrong? Like BlackBerry, they took the wrong risks. They failed to see the future. They let opportunity pass them by. The business that refuses to evolve with the world eventually finds itself in an environment in which it can't survive. While it may continue to limp its way through life, it's unlikely to ever regain its high standing in the market again. We've seen this happen time and time again. Let's discuss several cautionary tales.

Yahoo!

Once upon a time, Yahoo! was a dominant force on the internet. Launching in 1994, it was a multifaceted web portal, which included a directory-based search engine, that appeared in the right place at the right time. With few genuine competitors in the early days, it looked like nothing could ever stunt the company's growth.

Now, however, Yahoo! is but a distant memory in the minds of many. For others, it doesn't even register. Of course, the company still exists, but it's just a shadow of its former ubiquitous self.

The thing is, through acquisitions, Yahoo! could have remained one of the most dominant forces on the internet. In 2002, the company passed on the chance to purchase Google for a modest $1 billion. Considering Alphabet (Google) later reached a value of over $1 trillion, to put it bluntly, Yahoo! *really* fucked up. Apparently, the company didn't think its search engine was worth improving because it wasn't generating a lot of revenue at the time.[5] Sure, hindsight is 20/20, but the Yahoo! case is the perfect example of what failing to see the future and seize opportunity by the throat gets you: a quick trip to Obscurity Lane.

Kodak

Do you remember when Kodak was *the* camera brand? Sure, it had its competitors, such as Fujifilm, Nikon, and Canon, but, for a time, it seemed too big, too popular to fail. Of course, it did fail, filing for bankruptcy in 2012. So, what went wrong? Digital photography.

In this case, Kodak actually did its research, accurately predicting that digital photography would eventually disrupt the industry. Ironically, the company was responsible for many of the innovations in this area, but it made one fatal mistake: it chose to double down on the wrong technology. It decided it was primarily a film- and photochemical-based business, and digital was the enemy of its biggest source of revenue – a source that would inevitably, and quite naturally, dry up.[6]

Sigh. Kodak was like a car aimed at a telegraph pole with plenty of forewarning and time to steer back onto the road and avoid catastrophe altogether. In the case of digital photography, innovation wasn't risky; it was necessary and inevitable. Kodak's refusal to accept this fact, with countless opportunities to correct course, is what led to its slow-motion crash into obscurity.

Blockbuster

Blockbuster is another failed company that could have remained a dominant force had it not shunned innovation. In fact, when Netflix disrupted the industry, Blockbuster's then CEO, John Antioco, tried to alter the direction of the company. He proposed switching to a digital platform and doing away with the late fees that had plagued customers but driven profits. Unfortunately, the board disagreed with his direction and ousted him in 2005.

From there, Blockbuster suffered a slow and painful death, finally filing for bankruptcy in 2010.[7] Once again, a lack of innovation led to stagnation and, ultimately, the demise of another industry giant.

Clearly, Blockbuster had the resources to compete with industry disruptors, such as Netflix, but certain executives at the company were too short-sighted to understand that business as usual was the riskiest approach they could have taken.

These cautionary tales speak for themselves. When it comes to maintaining your innovative edge, the approach you take will depend on your unique situation. In some cases, internal innovation may be the solution. In others, a strategic acquisition may be the better choice. Either way, we should aim to avoid the mistakes of fallen giants at all costs. Let their failures be our lessons.

IT'S ALL-IN, OR IT'S NOTHING

When you found a startup, at some point, you'll either have to seize opportunity and take a calculated leap of faith or abandon the venture altogether. Without an all-in approach to business, which could mean quitting your day job, you'll struggle to reach the top tiers of success.

When I quit my well-paying job to focus solely on Tiliter, it probably looked like I was taking a massive risk. I was leaving stable employment, with only two weeks' salary in the bank, to found a startup tech company. To some, it seemed like a risky move. To others, it seemed totally insane. To me, it was a tough decision. We all know what I eventually chose to do, but it was a conversation with my father that gave me the final nudge I needed.

I explained what I wanted to do. "It's risky," I said.

My father paused in thought. "You're twenty-four years old," he finally said. "If there was ever an ideal time to give it a shot, it would be now. Really, you don't have a lot to lose."

"But I've worked hard to get to the position I'm in. I'd be giving it all up. Like I said, it's risky."

"Why couldn't you go back to doing what you're doing now? If you fail, what's stopping you from getting another good job at a good company?" He had a point. "Of course, I'd love to see you succeed, but you *can* afford to fail."

"You're right," I said, "but if I do this, failure isn't an option." *Failure isn't an option.* When I quit my job to focus on Tiliter, that's the attitude I brought to the company. While failure wouldn't ruin me completely, in my mind, it just wasn't an option.

From day one of making the decision, I went all-in and worked nonstop to make the business a success. Because I was practically broke, I had to make things happen as fast as possible, moving mountain after mountain. I don't think I even explained to my partner at the time how little money I had in the bank and how risky the decision was. Silly, perhaps, but I didn't need the doubt. I didn't need anyone trying to talk me out of it – because no one could have understood how driven I was to succeed. For me, success was non-negotiable, and the consequences of failure fuelled that mindset.

During Tiliter's early days, the risk-taking didn't slow down. Less than two years in, we had to quickly make a decision about expanding overseas. *Do we seize opportunity? Or do we let it pass by?* We got an offer to move the company to Germany, where English isn't the main language and we didn't know the culture. When we did a market analysis, we realised the market was bigger overseas, which is often the case. We knew we would have to expand beyond Australia at some point, and now we had an opportunity to do so. Naturally, we weighed up the risks against the rewards and tried to predict all possible outcomes. In the end, we decided the risk was worth the reward, so we sold all our gear, jumped on a plane, and moved to Germany. Yes, it was a risky move, but it was an exciting risk to take. Importantly, it was the right move to make.

I understood the direction the company needed to go, and I knew I could make it work. Ultimately, I knew what we had to do to win. Nowadays, before I invest in a startup, I ask this question: "How do you win?" Often, the path to winning involves moving mountains, redirecting rivers, and sometimes altering the very orbit of the Earth itself. But if you've got the drive to succeed and you're willing to seize opportunity when it presents itself, you'll make it happen – because failure won't be an option.

In business, you're going to experience tough moments. There are plenty of leaders out there who look great when their businesses are doing well but when the shit hits the fan, you'll find out who the real leaders are. As a startup founder, you'll be pushed to what you thought were your limits and beyond, and how you handle adversity will dictate whether your story is one of failure or success.

EVERYONE SHOULD HAVE A NEAR-DEATH EXPERIENCE, SORT OF...

How many near-death experiences does the average person experience before they're 40? I've had quite a few now, but I don't think it's the norm. Hey, I could be wrong. Either way, when you realise how quickly life – yours or someone else's – can be taken away, you start to think about where you are, and where you want to go, from a different angle. Your perspective changes and your priorities along with it. It's hard to focus on the things that ultimately don't matter when you realise how much they *really* won't matter when you're no longer drawing breath.

In 2021, I was on my way to work, and I stopped at a cafe for a coffee to kickstart the day. I placed my order and stepped outside to make a phone call while I waited for my drink. Because I was on the phone, I was fairly oblivious to what was happening around me. People hurried by on the footpath, and cars buzzed past on the road. Nothing out of the ordinary. Suddenly, I heard an almighty crash and looked up in time to see a car swing towards me and mount the curb. Before I could react, my legs were knocked out from under me, and I launched over the car, landing in a stunned heap on the footpath. Pain shot through my legs and lower back, and I couldn't stand. For a moment, I thought I was paralysed, but I soon realised that my hip was out of place. I managed to pop it back in and climb to my feet.

In the end, my injuries were fairly minor considering I had just been hit by a car and dumped onto solid concrete, hip first. Importantly, I was alive but if I had been standing forward one more step, I would have gone under the car instead of over it. I would be dead.

I went to hospital and was out within a day, alive and relatively well. I would be sore for a while, but I was still here. Although the adrenaline had worn off, the shock of what had happened – and what had *almost* happened – stayed with me.

When I was hit by that car, I wasn't doing anything risky or unusual, just waiting for a coffee, and it all could have ended for me right there on the footpath a few blocks from the office. It wasn't something I could have predicted; it wasn't something I could have stopped. Basically, it was a classic example of wrong place, wrong time. Thankfully, it wasn't worst place, worst time, because I was standing at least one step in the right direction – but it was a close call.

After that particular near-death experience, I started to reassess all aspects of my life, as one generally does after glimpsing the end. At the time, I was putting off having kids. While it was something I eventually wanted to do, I had so many other things demanding my attention, so, in my mind, it wasn't the right time. But what was I waiting for? If I kept putting it, and other life goals, off until I wasn't busy, I would never get anything done outside of work, work, work. The car knocked a bit of sense into me, and I became a lot less selfish, shifting more of my focus to others, including my partner, and their goals. So, for me, getting hit by a car was ultimately a positive experience.

Does everyone need to get hit by a car to set their priorities straight? Not at all. If you can visualise it, you don't need to experience it. That, I'm sure, must come as a huge relief. If you can imagine situations before they happen, it allows you to almost live those experiences. You don't need to get hit by a car if you can visualise the outcome of a near-death experience. Sounds great, right?

When I played football, we received a lot of coaching around visualisation. If you visualise what you're going to do before you do it, during the game executing becomes much easier because, in your mind, you've already done it. You know what to expect. Of course, what you visualise won't always match reality, but it gives you something to work with when you've not yet lived the experience. When you understand the possibilities, you're better equipped to make the right decisions to get the outcomes you want.

WHY I NEVER CELEBRATED SUCCESS, AND WHY YOU SHOULD

Before my 2021 near-death experience, I wasn't really celebrating any wins. I was living in the future, always focused on getting to that next level, and I rarely stopped to acknowledge what I had already achieved.

Part of the problem was that while others perceived me as quite successful, I wasn't even close to where I wanted to be. However, when that out-of-control car knocked my legs out from under me, it also knocked a new level of appreciation into me. I began to reflect on where I was and where I wanted to be. From there, I was able to determine the next steps I needed to take to be the person I wanted to be.

When I thought about it, some of my achievements were pretty impressive. My life was great. The future looked bright. Why hadn't I stopped to acknowledge these things sooner? Often, we get so caught up in life that we neglect to actually live it. We could be gone tomorrow, so why not celebrate today?

After a near-death experience, some people have the opposite reaction. They decide that if everything could end in an instant, nothing really matters. Why bother? Why put in the effort? Why celebrate the futility of life? That's a dark path to go down, and it doesn't resonate with me. If everything can end in an instant, to me, everything matters more. I want to create more of an impact, celebrate my wins, and keep pushing towards the future while it's still there.

Previously, one of the reasons why I struggled to celebrate a win was because I expected it to happen. I had visualised the outcome, and I had taken the steps I needed to get there. When you're constantly crunching the numbers and using mental models to map the future, success doesn't come as a surprise. You see it coming a mile away and by the time it arrives, you've already moved on to the next thing. That's why I struggled to celebrate wins – because they weren't wins; they were *expectations*.

To get myself to a place where I could celebrate my wins, I had to look at them in context. Yes, I expected them to happen, but getting to that point took a lot of hard work. Nothing is completely risk-free, and I could have had my expectations shattered on many occasions.

So, I've learnt that it's important to spend some time in the present and celebrate your wins or, at the very least, acknowledge the work you did to get there. Who knows? Tomorrow you could get hit by a car while waiting for coffee.

KEY TAKEAWAYS FROM CHAPTER 8

1. Know the answer to the question 'how do you win?'. This will set you apart from the majority of the competition and, even more importantly, be a reminder of what to focus on and what to leverage.

2. Celebrate wins. By celebrating your wins, you're setting a positive standard for your work processes. Remember, success breeds success.

3. Measure risk versus reward. Set a plan and take risk head-on. Those who are scared simply don't have a plan.

4. Exercise urgency in action. Recognise and act swiftly on opportunities before they disappear.

5. Live fully. Engage fully both in business and in your personal life, understanding that both are inherently temporary.

6. Take risks. Be willing to take calculated risks to capitalise on potential big gains.

7. Prioritise effectively. Balance the urgency of business actions with the importance of personal wellbeing and relationships.

PHILOSOPHY

9

PUT YOURSELF OUT THERE

NOTHING SELLS ITSELF

Has anyone ever tried to tell you that thing X sells itself? Well, it's bullshit. Nothing *ever* sells itself. How can something sell if no one knows it exists? If you want customers, you have to put yourself and your brand out there. You can't just create a product and hope the masses miraculously stumble upon it. Before people can convert to customers, they have to know about you and what you do.

To be successful, you have to build brand awareness; you have to build trust, and you have to build authority. If you don't, how can you expect people to care what you have to say? You need to get noticed, but how you get noticed is up to you. There are multiple avenues you can pursue, including clever marketing, word of mouth, or shouting your name from a mountain top. It doesn't so much matter *how* you put yourself out there, as long as people notice you – for the right reasons, of course. And to get people's attention, you have to make a bit of noise. Not only that, but you have to be confident in what you're doing. If you lack self-belief, putting yourself out there can be a daunting task. It's definitely something I struggled with in the beginning.

So, in this chapter, we'll discuss how to break through the noise and build brand awareness, the mindset you need to persuade investors to give you money, how to make your self-belief soar, and the fact that most people don't give a stuff about you or what you're doing. That last one may sound like a negative, but it's actually quite liberating to know that the majority of people couldn't care less about you or your business. It makes putting yourself out there a whole lot easier because you know you don't need to please everyone, not that you ever could.

BREAK THROUGH THE NOISE

How do you get your brand noticed? When I first stepped into the world of entrepreneurship, I had no idea how to put myself and my business out there. How do you get people talking about what you're doing? How do you catch their attention? How do you convert them into customers?

Look, I'm not going to try to cram an entire marketing course into this book. It wouldn't be practical, and it's not entirely relevant. Instead, I'll give you one piece of advice that will help you get noticed and gain traction in the beginning: you have to beat your own drum. You have to beat it *hard*. Until you've gained some notoriety, no one's going to be talking about you, your business, or your genius ideas. There's a lot of noise out there and if you want to be heard, you have to raise your voice. You have to loudly and proudly talk yourself up.

I know that's a bit of a douchey answer, but it's a fact of life. In Australia, we don't like to beat our own drums too much because, here, no one likes a bragger. However, in places like the United States, the culture is different. When I was working with startups in the US, I realised that a good amount of drum beating – or horn tooting – is not only expected, but it's practically mandatory if you want people to pay attention to what you're doing. You want to excite people, right? Then you can't beat your drum half-heartedly. You've got to put some effort into it. You've got to let people know exactly how good you are. Then, of course, you've got to deliver. Don't forget that part. If you make a claim, you need to back it up. Making over-the-top statements that you can't follow through on is a great way to lose the trust of your audience.

When you're putting yourself out there and trying to create brand awareness, you should be measuring the impact you're having, and you need to be deliberate in your approach. If you throw 100 darts at a dart board simultaneously to see what sticks, it's hard to measure exactly what worked and what didn't. If, instead, you take a more focused approach, throwing one dart at a time, it's much easier to measure and understand the impact of each toss. As with anything in business, when you're putting yourself out there, you can't ignore the numbers. They don't lie, and they'll let you know whether your approach is creating the impact you want or not. So, are you beating your drum in the best way possible?

The thing is, if your product is good, you won't have to beat your own drum for long. Eventually, others will start to do it for you. When third parties speak highly of you, two things happen. One, it takes the burden of drum beating off you, and, two, the drum beating is more effective. You can talk up yourself, your business, and your product, and you'll get some people's attention. But when someone else does it, especially someone with authority, people *really* start to listen. If you can build relationships with the right people and show *them* how great you are, they're going to tell others. They won't be able to help themselves. From there, it's a flow-on effect, and momentum will continue to build.

If you play the game well, you'll reach a point where your products talk for themselves. They won't *sell* themselves but once you've caught people's attention, if you're offering something amazing, selling becomes simple. The hard part is turning heads in the beginning, before you've positioned yourself as something worth looking at.

I know, if you haven't studied marketing, you may be hesitant to go out there and start making noise. Or if you're more of an introvert, like me, putting yourself out there is a daunting task.

But think of it like dating. If you're not putting yourself out there, the chances of the ideal partner falling into your lap are pretty low. To meet someone, there's no way around it – you have to put yourself out there, whether that means signing up to a dating app or actually leaving the house. You can't just sit at home, watching TV alone, and expect someone to walk through the door and demand a date. It's not how dating works, and it's not how business works. If you want to attract customers, investors, whoever, you have to put yourself out there. Period. Once they show some interest, well, that's when the wining and dining starts.

YOU WANT FUNDING? GET USED TO HEARING 'NO'

Some of the hardest people to (figuratively) get into bed are investors. Why wouldn't they be? They have a lot more to lose than the average customer. With that said, they also have a lot more to gain. Dealing with investors and securing funding is a big part of putting yourself out there as a founder. It can also be one of the most intimidating tasks you'll ever undertake.

Of course, investors want to find amazing startups to invest their money in. However, when they perform due diligence, they're generally looking for reasons *not* to invest in a business. They want to know exactly what they would be getting themselves into. What are the problems? What are the risks? Where are the holes? When they start asking these questions, you better have solutions; otherwise, you'll swiftly send investors walking the other way.

Generally, investors are looking out for their best interests. Would you expect anything less? So, you can't take rejection personally. For investors, it's all about risk mitigation – or, often, risk avoidance. Most don't need to take unnecessary risks when there's a safer, surer option waiting down the road.

When raising capital, you could meet with 100 or more investors and have each one tear your business apart. They're not trying to bring you down. Well, most aren't, anyway. They just want to ensure they make a good investment. If you come in with the mindset that investors are just doing their due diligence, you won't take it too personally. It can take hundreds of noes to get one yes and after rejection after rejection, you may start to question everything, which is understandable.

Like I said, investors are looking for reasons not to invest. If those same reasons keep coming up again and again, it's good feedback. Maybe they've identified something you missed. In which case, it might be something you can fix. If you can address their objections and plug any holes, you're several steps closer to getting that all-important 'yes'.

The trick is to separate opinion from genuine, useful feedback. As an entrepreneur, you're almost certainly doing something risky, and investors will recognise this. They're going to see *all* the risks involved, and some will offer great feedback, while others will only offer opinions, which are less useful. For example, someone might reject *your* opinion about what the future market is going to look like. It doesn't mean either of you are wrong, but you're both expressing an opinion. Sure, a lot of thought and research may have gone into forming that opinion, but it's not solid fact. It can't be proven.

However, if an investor were to say that your calculations on the total available market are incorrect – and they were right – that would be a tangible fact. You know they're not investing because the market isn't big enough. It's feedback you can take on board and a problem you can potentially solve.

Often, when you're trying to win investors over, opinions do come into play. It's the whole crazy or genius concept again. Some entrepreneurs who revolutionised entire industries were labelled crazy – until they proved they weren't. But it can also go the other way. Sometimes, so-called geniuses don't live up to the hype. They crumble and fall apart completely, and we're left wondering why we ever believed in them in the first place.

So, as always, when it comes to dealing with investors, it's important to sort fact from opinion. One can help you improve, while the other will only hold you back.

SPEAK LIKE THE WALLS HAVE EARS

The startup scene is a competitive landscape, and the way you communicate, both internally and externally, can either give you an edge or be a detriment to your success.

Firstly, you have to be your own salesperson. You have to be putting yourself out there – to customers, investors, the media – and touting the genius things you're going to do or are currently doing. Naturally, you should be as transparent as possible because you want to build trust with these groups, right? Transparency goes a long way to building a favourable profile for you and your business. It also demonstrates the type of leader you are. So, it's not just about putting yourself out there but also putting *the best version of you* out there.

I've seen stealth startups that have amazing, genius ideas but get nowhere because no one knows they exist. They're working away behind closed doors and have no public face. However, if they had just put themselves out there, a whole new market may have taken off. They could have been major success stories, but they never took the right steps. They didn't want to let anyone in behind the curtain, so they rose and fell, and no one even noticed.

Behind closed doors, every company is a shitshow. It's a fact. They each have their own challenges, problems, and failures to deal with, as will you. The difference is how you communicate this to customers, investors, and other stakeholders. If you're honest and upfront about the challenges you're facing, you'll gain a lot of respect from the market. The road to success is long, rough, and winding, so you need to build as much trust as possible along the way, including internal trust among your teams.

What you say externally should match the internal reality and culture of the business. Anything you say within the company should be okay to say publicly. I'm not saying you should shout your trade secrets from the rooftops, but the values you demonstrate internally should match those you're presenting to the outside world. I've seen companies that basically have two sets of values. They want their customers to see one thing on the surface, while the internal reality is a whole lot different. Eventually, those companies lose the trust of the public and potentially their staff when they notice the inconsistency. Once you go down the path of presenting a false face to the public, it's difficult to find your way back. In many cases, you would need to tear down and rebuild the entire company culture, which can be a disruptive process. So, you're better off getting it right from the beginning.

As a leader, you're the guiding light within your business, for better or worse – but preferably for the better. When your internal and external messages match, you leave no room for doubt in staff, customers, investors, stakeholders, and even yourself. Everyone knows exactly who you are and what you stand for.

KEY TO STOKING SELF-BELIEF

When you're suffering from self-doubt, community is everything. The people you surround yourself with are so important. The right people will lift you up, enhance you, and propel you forward, and you'll do the same for them. As we know, success breeds success. If you're a solo entrepreneur, having an amazing community to bounce ideas off and seek advice from is even more important. You don't need to go it alone.

When you lack self-belief, putting what you're doing into context can allay any doubts, and community helps with this. If you're working in a bubble, isolated from your peers, context is difficult to gain. You can't really know how well you're going in comparison, which can fuel self-doubt. You might be absolutely killing it, but your own expectations are so high that you think you're failing. A good community will let you know when you're winning – and maybe help you celebrate those wins – and offer advice when you're not.

I do have a disclaimer to add. Ideally, you should diversify the types of people you hang around with. If you're only engaging with people who are at your level and doing similar things to you, you're only hearing from one segment of society. On top of that, it can get competitive when you're all working in the same space, vying for success. It's not that there's not enough success to go around, but entrepreneurs are naturally driven to win, and it sometimes presents in less than favourable ways.

That's why I love going back to my rural home town and catching up with people who have taken completely different paths to me. We'll catch up for a coffee or beer and chat about what we've been doing since we last spoke. Of course, they react positively to what I've done, which helps with self-belief. I'm getting validation, in a sense, from outside sources.

Granted, you shouldn't need the validation of others to believe in yourself, but a little reminder here and there that you're doing some pretty cool stuff doesn't hurt. Sometimes, as entrepreneurs, we forget where we started, how far we've come, and how great it is that we get to do what we do. But the right people will remind you when you need to hear it most.

YOU'RE NOTHING TO MOST PEOPLE

It might be tough to hear, but most people don't give a stuff about you or what you do. They don't care if you win, lose, succeed, or fail. You're not the centre of the Universe. Yes, you may be the centre of *your* universe, but you're not the centre of anyone else's. The sooner you accept this, the sooner you'll start making better decisions. If you waste time and energy trying to impress or cater to people who don't care, you're not going to produce results that resonate with you or your actual audience.

When it comes to your entrepreneurial peers, most of them won't care about you or your goals either. Everyone is running their own race, and they don't have time to think about you. It's a question we often ask ourselves when we first start putting ourselves out there: *What do people think?* The answer – most people aren't thinking about you at all. They simply don't care.

Of course, you should surround yourself with plenty of people who *do* care, but most entrepreneurs you meet in the wild aren't interested in you in a significant way. If someone does start to show an unusual level of interest, they may have ulterior motives, for better or worse. They may see you as the competition and are digging for inside information, or they may want to invest. You'll need to determine what their intentions are.

The Earth holds billions of people, and there are a lot of us out there doing a lot of different things. To most people, you mean absolutely nothing – and that's great. It should come as a relief, a huge weight lifted off your shoulders. Now you're free to focus on what matters to you. You're not out to impress the masses. You're here to make the impact *you* want to make, even if it can only ever be small in the grand scheme of things. The Universe, after all, is a big place.

1. It's not enough to have an idea. It's not even enough to create. You have to be able to sell. Most of what you're doing is selling. Because if you're not, how are you getting things out there? How are you actually making a difference? How are you creating value?

2. You're not the centre of the Universe. The moment you understand this is the moment you can truly live freely in what you do. It's the freedom to talk and act in a way that means something to you and is not to impress others.

3. Transparency goes a long, long way. Talking and presenting values, ideas, reporting, and so on in the same way both internally and externally is an extremely powerful way to do business.

4. Visibility matters. The more people know about you and your business, the more opportunities you will encounter.

5. Networking is crucial. Build and maintain relationships that can provide support, advice, and opportunities.

6. Focus on personal branding. Develop and promote a personal brand that aligns with your business values and vision.

7. Engage publicly. Actively participate in industry events, social media, and public discussions to increase your visibility.

PHILOSOPHY

10

MASTER YOUR MINDSET – FROM STARTUP TO SCALING

MINDSET MASTERY 101

Many of us don't treat the mind like we do any other part of the body. We care for our physical selves with diet, rest, and exercise, but not all of us regularly care for our minds.

One thing we can all do for ourselves is have a therapist we talk to on a regular basis, even when things are going well. When you're going to the gym, you don't stop because you start getting results. In fact, you might even start going more often and pushing harder. The more you go, the better the results, and you start to get good at getting those results.

We don't always do this for the mind. Often, we don't seek a professional until we absolutely need one, and when we're at that stage, we can struggle to make the progress we need. Or perhaps we can't find the right person to help us get to where we want to be. Really, you should be training the mind like you would a muscle. You want it to be strong and functional when you need it.

As an entrepreneur, you're going to experience stress, overwhelm, and, in some cases, utter disaster, so you need to make sure you're mentally ready to handle adversity. You know the road ahead is going to be tough, so taking a preventative approach to mental health is far better than trying to learn to swim *after* the water has started to rise.

In business, we use a lot of mental models to try to predict the future. Mainly, we want to know what could go wrong. However, we rarely do this on a personal level. I'm not saying we should dwell on worst-case scenarios, but we *can* predict likely outcomes and prepare for them. When a negative event doesn't come as a complete surprise, mentally it's much more manageable.

So, in this chapter, we'll dive into the topic of mastering your mindset. Prevention is better than cure, and you can put systems in place now that will make the journey from startup to scaling and beyond a whole lot easier. We'll discuss the differences between stress and burnout, the power of asking the right questions, why self-development is bullshit, how to build highly functional teams, and the value of taking a break. That's right, you are allowed to take a holiday every now and then. In fact, the long-term success of your business demands it.

STRESS VS. BURNOUT – TWO VERY DIFFERENT BEASTS

One of the biggest things I hear from founders is, "I'm so burnt out." Burnout can be catastrophic, and it certainly does happen, but there's a big difference between feeling stressed and being burnt out. The problem is that some people lump them into the same category. They might be feeling tired and overworked, so they say they're burnt out. If you're tired, a good night's sleep might be the cure. If you're overworked, it might be time to take a holiday. However, if you're genuinely burnt out, you're in the danger zone, and relighting the fire may not be easy or, in some cases, possible.

When you pour every part of yourself into your business, you're going to feel stressed and tired at times. If you've got other commitments outside of work, such as kids, you're going to feel the pressure even more. Often, the solution is simply better time and energy management, which we'll discuss later.

Burnout is a different beast. When you're burnt out, you feel numb. You lose interest in what you're creating. You may not even want to get out of bed in the morning. Mentally, you start to disconnect from the work you're doing, from the business, from the people around you. Basically, you stop caring.

When you're stressed, generally you're still eager to keep working. You still have that energy and drive. You're feeling the pressure, and you can still perform. Being overworked or overburdened can take a physical toll. You may feel tired; your nutrition may suffer because you're not eating properly, or you may not have time to go to the gym. Generally, you can change certain things in your life to correct course: reduce your work hours, take a longer lunch break, go to bed earlier, make time for exercise, whatever you need to do. Like I said, it's usually just a matter of better managing your time and energy. Simple, right? Not always, I know.

For me, exercise is important, but I was struggling to find time to hit the gym, so I took up golf. Why golf? Because I could do business and exercise at the same time. It was a game changer for me because I was utilising my time well, getting outside in the fresh air, and doing something I enjoyed. If you find the right outlet for your stress, it won't build up inside and send you into burnout mode.

Hopefully, this never happens but when you do reach the burnout phase, the passion and drive are gone, which can be terrifying for a lot of people. How much are you going to achieve when you don't even want to get out of bed? How far can you go when you don't want to take another step? How can you possibly continue to run a business when you can't summon the energy to care anymore? You might have investors, shareholders, staff relying on you to show up every day, and you don't even want to be there. Once you fall into that pit, getting out without making some drastic life changes is near-impossible. The key is to never fall in in the first place.

Self-awareness of where you're at is important. If you feel like you're heading into burnout territory, you need to reroute immediately. Whenever I've been close to that point, I've found hobbies or activities I could use to close off my mind from work and focus on something else. For me, being able to switch off was important because when I strolled back into the office, I was able to *really* switch on. As entrepreneurs, we're tempted to carry our work around with us at all times – in our heads, in our laptops, in our phones – but that approach isn't sustainable long-term. You have to be able to figuratively switch yourself off and literally switch off those work devices if you hope to avoid burnout town. If you're someone who enjoys being 'on' 24/7 and can't imagine ever burning out, that's great, but most people don't fall into that category. We need to disconnect. We need our downtime. We need to live lives outside of the hustle of entrepreneurship.

Burnout doesn't only occur when you're stressed and things are going badly. It may sound counterintuitive, but you can still get burnt out when things are going well. You could be working hard, hitting milestones, and ascending to the summit of success, and you could still be heading into the burnout phase. So, whether things are going good or bad, you need to be conscious of what you're experiencing and head burnout off well before it hits.

ASK THE RIGHT QUESTIONS, GET THE RIGHT ANSWERS

When it comes to mindset management, as a founder, you're often not just managing your mindset but those of your teams as well. It's a big burden to carry, I know, but by asking the right questions, you can learn how people are travelling and whether they're on the road to burnout town.

Having regular one-on-one sessions with people is important. You should also monitor their workload, effort, and performance. With the right tools and by asking the right questions, you can understand whether people are overworking themselves, making too many sacrifices in their personal lives, or experiencing too much stress, and you can head off potential burnout before it becomes a problem.

One of the best things any leader can do is ask questions. You can't just tell people what to do and expect everything to go smoothly. Communication is a two-way street, and asking questions benefits everyone. You can't educate your teams if you don't understand the people in them and what they're experiencing. It's not only about asking questions but asking the *right* questions. Let me explain.

I was on a road trip with my father, travelling from Sydney to Perth. As we drove through the middle of the desert, we came to a small town. At this point, we knew where we were trying to go, but we didn't know which road would take us there, so we pulled over and asked one of the locals, who was walking along the street.

"Can we get to Cobar via that road?" we asked, pointing to the road we thought would take us to our destination.

"Yeah, sure," he said, "that road will take you to Cobar."

So, we thanked him and headed down the road we now knew would take us to our next stop. Back then, Google Maps wasn't really a thing, so we were relying on paper maps and the advice of locals, which had worked well up until that point.

As we drove, the road got a little more rugged than we expected, but we were in a four-wheel drive, so we weren't concerned. We kept going. We had, after all, been assured that this road would take us to our destination. Why would that man lie to us? What would he have to gain? Eventually, the road got so rough that it was barely a road anymore. At that point, we knew we weren't on the best route to our stop. On top of that, we were close to running out of fuel.

"What was that guy's problem?" I asked, as we bounced along the dirt not-road.

Dad laughed. "It wasn't his fault. It's on us. We asked the wrong question."

"What do you mean?"

"We asked if we could get to Cobar via this road. We didn't ask if this was the *best* road to get there. Based on what we asked, his answer was correct."

Dad was right. Eventually, we did get there, keeping the vehicle alive with spare fuel from our jerry cans. We rolled into town, running on fumes, and feeling a little foolish about what had happened. Lesson learnt.

If you ask the right questions, you'll get the right answers, and then you can act accordingly based on the information you have. If you do this regularly, you'll understand your teams, the problems they're facing, and what you can do to help.

Also, when you do take action, you need to get a feedback loop happening as fast as possible. When the road got rough, we should have realised we weren't on the typical route to our destination. Ideally, based on the feedback we were receiving – an unmaintained road – we would have pieced it all together and turned back. The same applies when managing a team. You should be able to get good feedback loops and make adjustments where necessary.

That day, I learnt a valuable lesson about asking the right questions to get the information I needed. If you're not careful with your questioning – and your listening – you could end up going down a shitty road and almost getting stranded in the desert. And no one wants that.

IS IT OKAY TO VENT?

Fostering healthy teams is great, but you also need to look after your own mental health. As entrepreneurs, especially if we're doing it solo, we can shoulder a lot of the burden of running the business. Ideally, we should have people we can share the burden with. At the very least, we need people we can vent to.

As a founder, as an entrepreneur, who can you talk to when things get tough? Who can you seek advice from? Who can you vent to? As a leader, you're expected to be positive all the time. You're the rock that everyone else in the company leans on when times get tough. I've tried being honest with my teams when I'm stressed about something, and it always backfires. They think, *If he's worried, then I should be worried too*, and you end up stressing out the people around you. You have to be mindful of the energy you're putting out because people feed off that. If you're constantly being super negative, your team is going to adopt that same mindset.

I'm not going to name any names, but there are plenty of successful people who take out their frustrations on their teams. They become cruel and abusive because that's their outlet for stress. What sort of environment do you think that creates? Sure, many of these people *are* successful. But are they fulfilled? If you're constantly attacking the people around you, you're probably not living an enjoyable life. Personally, I think there's a better way.

For me, getting housemates again for a period of time was the answer. At the end of the day, we would all be at home, discussing what we'd been doing. It was great to vent, to get my problems off my chest, and to hear other people's struggles. We all have problems; they're an unavoidable part of life, and we need ways to alleviate the stress that accompanies them. Venting to my teams would have ruined morale, but my housemates weren't connected to the business or what I was doing. They could listen, perhaps offer some words of encouragement, and move on. They didn't get bogged down in my problems, and I didn't dwell on theirs. But now we all had people to vent to, and it absolutely helped.

You need to have someone who you can be real with. Unless you're running a multi-founder organisation, you can't expect other people in the business to understand what you're going through. Now, I'm not saying you shouldn't be open and honest with your teams. Generally, leaders who are more transparent have better functioning teams, but that doesn't mean you should dump your problems on other people in the workplace. They're not going to understand, and you're only going to bring them down.

Venting is fine, as long as you're venting to the right people. You don't want to create more problems for yourself or others. As entrepreneurs, we're in the business of solving problems, not creating them.

THE BIGGEST SELF-DEVELOPMENT TRICK OUT THERE

Entrepreneurs are always looking for the next new trick, whether it be for money, marketing, or mindset. But here's the trick – there is no next trick. It's hard to hear, I know. In the beginning, a lot of entrepreneurs learn some good tactics to get them started, gain momentum, and earn some success, but they eventually hit a plateau and find themselves asking, *All right, what's next?* Where does that lead them? Down the bottomless rabbit hole of self-development.

Of course, that hole *is* full of tricks, but there are millions of them, and most of them only work when you're new to the game. When you don't know what you're doing, anything that gives you an edge seems like magic. But once you become competent, the tricks lose their lustre and don't appear as effective.

I see so many founders looking for the next big thing. They want a shortcut to further success – but there are no shortcuts. One trick isn't going to solve all, or even any, of your problems. You can waste a lot of time and money on self-development and not move the dial at all. When all the practical tricks fail, people generally turn to the more mystical options.

On their quest for answers, they start focusing on mindfulness, manifestation, and going to retreats. But they don't find what they're looking for in these things either. They're still stressed; they're still confused; they still feel unfulfilled, so they jump onto the next trend, repeating the cycle over and over.

I'm not saying you can't get some benefits from the spiritual side of self-development, but the real trick is that there is no trick. Once you accept and understand this, you're free to focus on what *will* actually help your business, your mindset, and your life. In this book, I don't offer quick tricks or simple solutions. How could I? Every business, every person is different, and what works for one might not work for another. Instead, I offer insights, observations, and philosophies I've found to be true. What you do with them is up to you. You can spend years absorbing bucketloads of advice, but only you can determine what's relevant to you and your business. You shouldn't action anything without asking yourself, *Is this right for me?* You shouldn't action *any* advice without giving it some serious thought; that includes the advice in this book.

BUILDING HIGHLY FUNCTIONAL TEAMS

Let's talk team building. Firstly, every organisation is different, and every founder varies in the way they like to set up and manage their teams.

Personally, I back my team members completely so if I hire someone, I want to be 100 percent sure they can not only execute but execute without me. I also hire people who are smarter than me. Those are the people you want, yeah? If not, you might as well just do it all yourself.

Ideally, you don't want to be micromanaging. When you really start to scale, you literally won't have time to micromanage everyone. Instead, you should offer support when employees need it. You want to trust your team to get the job done, and you don't want to get in their way. Of course, it all comes down to asking the right questions and ensuring you're offering the right support.

Basically, my management style is to let people run loose and do whatever they want. Then, once a fortnight, we have a one-on-one, where, naturally, I ask the right questions and listen to what they have to say.

"How can we make this happen?"

"What do you need to move forward?"

"What support can I provide?"

If I understand what they need, I can provide the right support, and shit generally gets done. As long as you've hired the right people, it's a pretty effective and stress-free way to manage a team. That is, stress-free for both sides. They're happy and productive because I'm not constantly standing behind them, cracking the whip, correcting every move, and I'm happy for the same reasons – because I don't want to be doing that stuff.

When it comes to setting up teams, I've found that it's always easier to start fresh than it is to absorb a team from another company. If you're in the acquisition game, you can't really avoid the latter, and you're likely going to end up laying off a lot of people before everything is running smoothly. As you scale and bring people into the company, you should frequently ask yourself, *Who can I trust?* Ideally, it should be everyone you hire.

When building teams, I'm also aiming to remove founder dependency. If I get hit by a bus – or car while waiting for coffee – the show must go on. So, how can you set up your teams so they're not dependent on you? If there's something you're deeply engaged in within the business, how can you ensure it can continue in a meaningful way without you?

The same goes for team members as well. How can you remove dependency on them? As you move forward, there should be no points of failure. If someone leaves, it shouldn't affect momentum or cripple the business. When you remove dependencies, you also make everyone's jobs easier and less stressful. If someone needs to take time off, they know they can. Someone else will jump in and keep their seat warm while they're away. Basically, you want to build a machine where every part is replaceable, but you also want to ensure that you always have all the spare parts you need on hand.

If you've hired the right people and plugged all the holes – that is, filled any skill gaps – most of team management is more about managing people on a personal level than it is about managing their jobs. Even though I referred to employees as replaceable parts in a machine, they're much more than that, and they each need to be supported in different ways.

IT'S TIME TO STEP DOWN FROM YOUR IVORY TOWER

When you're a founder, you can end up being insulated from aspects of the business that don't require your direct attention, which is natural. You don't want to spend your time answering customer queries, packing orders, or cleaning windows when you've hired people to do these things so you can focus on what you do best. But if you don't understand what every part of the machine is doing, you can't understand the machine as a whole. Importantly, you can't give each person or team in the business the support they need.

So, I think it's crucial to spend time in each area of the company, asking the right questions, listening, and figuring out how you can make things better. I'm not saying you should spend a month answering phones or whatever the job might be, but you should take time to understand what each team is experiencing.

For example, when I became CEO of startup community Fishburners, I spent a week sitting on the front desk during the early mornings, checking people in, and trying to understand the processes. Without doing that, I could never have fully understood the experience of the front desk staff. To gain that understanding, I had to insert myself into the action. When you intimately understand the processes in place, you're no longer making theoretical decisions. The decisions you make will be practical, and I guarantee your employees will appreciate it.

There's also the added bonus of creating transparency. If you're out there, experiencing the realities of each role within the business, team members can't hide behind processes after something goes wrong. And if you're out there seeing it all firsthand, they also can't hide when something *is* going wrong. You can't do everything, and you can't be everywhere at all times, but a little awareness goes a long way.

MANAGE TIME AND ENERGY LIKE A PRO

Everything I do is quite calculated. Internally, in all of my companies, I've used the OKR (objectives and key results) method to ensure that everything I'm doing is working towards the objectives we have as a business. Once you know your goals, your results will tell you if you're on the right track or if you need to adjust course. When you're deliberate and methodical in your approach, you ensure that you're channelling your time and energy in the right direction.

That's why it's important to make sure you're measuring output by using the right tools, creating the right documentation, and, importantly, focusing on the things that matter. There's no point wasting time and resources measuring metrics that don't relate to your objectives. Instead, you should measure the things that will take you to your goals.

Often, people will compile a bunch of KPIs that look good on paper but have no correlation to the objectives of the business. Are the things you're measuring relevant to your six-month, one-year, and five-year goals? If not, you need to ask yourself why you're focusing on those metrics. If you don't have a good reason, you're sending your energy in the wrong direction.

When you understand the numbers, managing your time and energy becomes much easier. You know which actions will be the most impactful, so you can direct your effort in that direction. However, if you're focusing on the wrong statistics, you can end up working hard for the sake of working hard, which happens a lot more than you might think. It's like running on a treadmill. Yes, you might be burning calories, but you're not actually getting anywhere.

When your goals are clearly defined, you know where to channel your energy, and it helps you and everyone else stay focused on the right things. There's nothing worse for morale and energy management than continually changing objectives. If you keep switching people's focus, they'll feel like they're never getting anything done, and they will, quite literally, never get anything done. When people start projects, they want to see them through to completion and witness the outcome. If you're constantly redirecting their focus, they don't get the satisfaction of completion or seeing the results of their hard work.

Instead, they feel like they're on that treadmill, sweating hard but getting nowhere.

So, when it comes to managing time and energy, it's all about the numbers. The numbers never lie.

A LOVE LETTER TO THE NUMBERS

Did you think I was done talking about numbers? I'm not letting you off that easily. In the beginning, a lot of entrepreneurs aren't interested in the statistics. There's nothing sexy about a spreadsheet. Well, depending on who you ask. When you're first starting out, the numbers aren't going to tell you what you want to hear. In fact, they're going to be brutally honest. If the business isn't performing, the numbers will let you know, which can be disheartening to many of us. However, the statistics show you where you need to improve and, eventually, how far you've come. How are you going to know if you're gaining traction if you aren't measuring anything? Intuition will only get you so far.

Ideally, if you're not a numbers person, you need someone in your team who is, whether that's a co-founder or someone else. You need to be logical when making decisions, and using numbers to guide you helps remove emotion from the equation.

As an entrepreneur, this can be a difficult way to operate. Often, we're so invested in the problem we want to solve that we can't help but let our emotions influence our actions. It gets personal; it becomes a part of your identity, and you put everything into finding a solution. When you're in that frame of mind and the numbers aren't telling you what you want to hear, you might take offence and decide the numbers are bullshit. But the numbers are there to guide you, not hinder you, and you can't ignore them and expect to reach the highest levels of success.

From a finance perspective, you *absolutely* can't ignore the numbers. At the bare minimum, you need to understand the basics and if you're going for investment, you need to understand a whole lot more. If you're not measuring these things, they don't exist. You could be out there doing amazing things but if there's no documentation, there's no proof. Do you expect an investor to just take you on your word? It's not how it works. Like I said, the numbers don't lie and if you're out there killing it, they're going to support you. Ultimately, the numbers are your friend.

YOU HAVE PERMISSION TO TAKE A BREAK

When I went all-in as an entrepreneur, I didn't take a holiday for six years. I don't recommend this to anyone. Was I successful? Sure, maybe. Could I have been successful *and* taken a break every now and then? Absolutely. Unfortunately, there's often a stigma around founders doing anything but hustling 24/7, in the beginning, at least. Every hour you work pushes you an inch closer to success, so you can't afford to slow down, rest, or even sleep a lot of the time – or so we think.

We've all heard the phrase "work smarter, not harder." Well, you can work smart *and* hard and achieve a lot more. Granted, you need to work hard to gain that initial momentum, but you've also got to be smart about it. I guarantee that if I had taken the occasional break, my output would have been much better. If your teams are set up well, you *should* be able to take time off without everything burning down.

Once again, the ability for a founder to take a holiday comes down to removing dependencies. The quicker you can do this, the better your business will run. Once you've started to scale and have some teams in place, if you still feel like you can't take a break, that's a clear sign that something is wrong. I wish I had learnt this sooner.

Eventually, I realised that dependencies were an issue for my business. They were holding us back and, quite frankly, burning some of us out. So, we made some changes, and I took a short holiday overseas. The problem was, it wasn't much of a holiday at all. Of course, I was fully contactable the entire time, and the other co-founders would call me as if I were still in the office, bringing my mind back to work. I couldn't switch off, and I couldn't relax. Looking back, I was pretty close to burnout at that stage, and I needed the break. I needed a *real* break, not a working holiday. I needed to totally switch off from the business, which is okay to do, as long as you've removed those dependencies.

As a founding group or as a team, you have to be open and honest with one another about where you're at, what you're feeling, and what you need. If someone needs a break, give them a break, a *real* break.

The ability for the founder – and anyone in the business – to take time off is a sure sign that you're doing something right. You should be looking to remove all dependencies as soon as possible so when you do want to take a holiday, you can, minus the doubt. *Will the business survive without me?* If the answer is 'no', it's time to make some changes.

We often get stuck on the idea that the harder you work, the more successful you'll be. But it's not true. You may increase your chances of success, sure. As we know, success is more about focusing your time and energy on the *right* things, not just running on the entrepreneurial treadmill, burning calories for no significant gain. From a time and energy perspective, impact is way more important than input.

As a leader, a founder, a CEO, your team doesn't want you working yourself to the bone, never eating, and rarely sleeping. Instead, they want you to see around corners. They need you to predict what's coming so they and the business can be ready. But when you're neck-deep in every part of the company, it's hard to get clarity. When you're too close to everything, it's difficult to see the bigger picture and make the right decisions.

So, you have permission to take a break. In fact, you owe it to yourself and your business. Even us seemingly tireless entrepreneurs need some downtime every now and then. With that said, don't take the piss. What do I mean? I've seen founders exaggerate their workload to justify a holiday or time off. Guess what? Most of them fail. As a busy founder, your time management will never be perfect. I doubt there are any great leaders or successful people who manage their time perfectly, getting a solid eight hours sleep every night and never missing a commitment. While you can't perfectly manage your time, you can manage it strategically, which means taking a break when you need it.

1. Asking the right questions can be the difference between success and failure. Think carefully about what you actually ask because it will dictate the answers you receive, which will ultimately shape your decisions.

2. Know when and who you can vent to. Ensure you aren't creating chaos – but don't bottle it up!

3. Understand your capacity, your team's capacity, and the work ahead. Plan for everything well in advance and don't be a worry wart. You can't stay in your job forever. It's impossible, quite frankly. One day, you'll die, and you certainly can't be there then. So, do the work to remove dependencies.

4. Fewer team members who are amazing are far better than more team members who are average. These people will multiply the good, while the average will multiply the bad.

5. Understand what gives you energy. Feel when you are getting low, or feeling high, be self-aware, and adjust your management accordingly.

6. Adopt a growth mindset. Embrace challenges and setbacks as opportunities for growth.

7. Practise adaptability. Be prepared to pivot and adapt strategies as the business grows and market conditions change.

8. Never stop learning. Commit to lifelong learning to remain competitive and innovative.

9. Develop leadership skills. Evolve your leadership style to meet the changing needs of your organisation as it grows.

PHILOSOPHY

11

MEANINGFUL RELATIONSHIPS ARE ONE OF YOUR STRONGEST ASSETS

RELATIONSHIPS COME IN MANY DIFFERENT FLAVOURS

Not all relationships are created equal, and the people in our lives all sit at different levels in the relationship hierarchy. We have acquaintances, friends, family, close friends, best friends, and partners, to name a few in no particular order. I genuinely believe that meaningful relationships make a world of difference in all aspects of our lives. Rather than having hundreds of shallow connections, we should aim to create deep relationships that become our strongest assets.

I've chosen to leave meaningful relationships until the final chapter. Why? Because relationships make the world go round. They're the pillars that hold up everything else. They're the secret to success. Without them, we wouldn't get far in business; we wouldn't get far in life.

So, in this chapter, we'll discuss the art of building, maintaining, and evaluating relationships and why meaningful connections are your biggest asset. Nothing else can compare.

IS IT MEANINGFUL?

How do you know where a relationship sits on the connection spectrum? How do you know when someone has moved from acquaintance to friend? How do you know whether a relationship is meaningful or superficial?

A good way to gauge it is to answer the question: Can you give person X a call at any time? When you're at that level, you know there's a certain amount of trust and friendship between you. It's not just a perfunctory or superficial relationship between colleagues or peers. There's a little more involved.

As an entrepreneur, you're going to meet a lot of amazing people: other entrepreneurs, CEOs, absolute geniuses. You'll talk to them at events, perhaps get some photos together, but, at the end of the day, a lot of those relationships will be quite shallow. You won't be able to call these people for a chat at any time – and that's okay. Not all of your relationships can be at that level, nor should you want them to be. We can only handle so many meaningful relationships at any given time. We don't want to overload ourselves now, do we?

To determine whether you've reached the next stage of a relationship, you should answer this question: What do we talk about? If your conversations are purely business-related, you're likely still at the phone buddy stage. Yes, you can call them any time, but you're not familiar with each other's personal lives in a meaningful way. When you can call someone about your personal as well as your business life, you know you've reached the next stage of the relationship. But wait – there's one more level after that.

If you think a relationship is truly meaningful, a true friendship, you can find out for sure by answering this question: Can you ask that person a favour without them expecting anything in return? If the answer is yes, congratulations, you've got a meaningful relationship on your hands. If, however, you know you would be in favour debt, you're still at the more superficial level, which is fine. You need all sorts of different people in your life. It's all about balance.

It's also important to note that just because you're at that level with someone, it doesn't mean you need to be in contact with them every day, every week, or even every month. When you have a meaningful relationship with someone, it doesn't matter how much time has passed since you last spoke because you're both there for each other regardless. You can see someone every day – at work, for example – and still have a really shallow relationship with them. Time spent together isn't a great indicator of the depth of a connection. It's more about the effort you're both investing in the relationship.

BUILDING MEANINGFUL RELATIONSHIPS, ONE BRICK AT A TIME

When building meaningful relationships, it's important to remember that they all start off at a more superficial level. Reaching the 'favour with no strings attached' stage takes time and effort. You have to nurture the relationship to reach that level.

The best way to kickstart any relationship is to go in without an agenda. You're not trying to get something from someone, and ideally they're not trying to get anything from you. You're just two people building a connection. One of our first investors at Tiliter came from a relationship like this. We simply met, had a lot of similar interests, and got to know each other over time. We never approached him for investment, but eventually he came to me and asked, "How do I invest?" At this stage, I could call him for anything, either personal or business-related. He's a friend, someone I can lean on, but we didn't reach this level overnight. Although the relationship grew organically, it didn't happen without effort on both our parts. You can't neglect to nurture a relationship and expect the other person to step up when you need them.

It may sound cliché, but you get out what you put in. This is especially true for relationships. The thing is, if you're going in with no agenda, you can't *expect* to get out what you put in. If you're nurturing a relationship because you want something from that person, well, that's not really a meaningful relationship, is it? It's more on the superficial level.

Transparency is key. If you want something from someone, be open and upfront about it from the outset. If someone asks me to grab a coffee but doesn't make their intentions clear, I get suspicious. If, instead, they're direct and open from the start, I'm more likely to agree to meet them. They might want something from me, or they might say, "There's no agenda, I just want to chat and get to know you," which is better than leaving me guessing.

You can't force a meaningful relationship. If you have an agenda, make it clear. If you don't have an agenda, make that clear too. By being transparent, you build immediate trust, and, in business and in life, there's no greater currency.

TRUST IS THE ULTIMATE CURRENCY

Whenever you're putting yourself out there, whether publicly or in relationships, building trust should always be the goal. You want people to trust you, your product, and your business.

Honestly, if there's no trust in a relationship, I just cut that person off. We all have limited time, energy, and mental resources, and investing in a relationship that's unlikely to be beneficial to either party is a waste. Would you want to confide in someone you don't trust? Would you buy a product you don't trust? Would you want to invest in a company you don't trust? Of course not. That's why trust is the ultimate currency. It buys you everything you could ever want: relationships, customers, capital. Trust is the key to everything.

If you're authentic in your relationships and in business, you're going to generate that trust organically. You won't have to force it or fight for it. Instead, it will naturally build over time, through transparency and competence. See, it's one thing to be honest with people, but you also have to prove you know what you're doing. You could be quite transparently wasting investors' money, but honesty will only get you so far. People want to know that you're competent in what you're doing. Competency is a big component of building trust.

Once you've built trust within your relationships, with investors, with your audience, whoever it might be, you need to ensure that you maintain that trust. You can spend years reaching a point where people are backing you 100 percent, and you could throw it all away in an instant. Sure, you can regain people's trust, but you're better off not losing it in the first place.

NEVER LIE. PERIOD

As a founder, it's hard to be transparent all the time. Beneath the shiny bonnet of most startups, it's an absolute shitshow. You don't really want people to know how chaotic things are behind the scenes, but, at the same time, you want to build trust. So, what do you do?

There's one primary philosophy I live my life by, and it hasn't failed me yet: never lie. "Honesty is the best policy" is absolutely a cliché, but the phrase has stuck around for a reason.

If you do find yourself taking a less than honest approach to business, relationships, or life in general, it's time to ask yourself some serious questions. Why are you choosing to lie? What do you expect to gain? What can you expect to lose? You should work backwards and figure out why you made the decision to lie. Was it absolutely necessary? (Hint – the answer is always 'no'). Could you have found a better way? (Hint – the answer is always 'yes'). What were the series of events that led to you making that decision, and how can it be avoided in the future?

When you're always transparent, a type of emotional intelligence forms, and you're able to work with people in more meaningful ways. Life actually gets easier when you're honest. For example, I've had people reach out for coffee, and I've told it to them straight: "Hey, I only have so much time and energy. Is this about something we can work on, or is it just for a chat?" I know how important managing my time and energy is, so I can't jump at every opportunity to sit down and talk, but I also don't want to waste time – mine or theirs – making excuses and leading them on. I've been told I'm too direct, but isn't that better than the alternative? When you're unreservedly honest with people, at least they know where they stand. Isn't that better than leaving them guessing? I think so.

It's one of the reasons why many entrepreneurs become dicks (or are perceived that way). They've learnt to be direct because it's the best way to navigate their busy lives. Who's going to take offence to honesty? Well, people who don't like what you have to say. But isn't it better to just say it anyway? When you're direct and honest, you save yourself a lot of hassle.

With that said, you can be direct *and* tactful at the same time. For instance, someone once asked me what I do when I'm at an event, stuck in a conversation that's going nowhere. A lot of people make excuses to leave: going to the toilet, getting a drink, stepping outside for some fresh air. But why make excuses? Instead, I usually say something like, "It was really nice to meet you. Perhaps we can pick this up another time." That way, I'm removing myself from the conversation, but I'm not scrambling for a bullshit excuse to leave. When you're in this situation, you don't owe anyone an explanation. If you're done with the conversation, you can make it clear without making excuses and, generally, without offending anyone. It's not like you're saying, "Mate, give it a rest. You're boring me to tears. How about you try not talking for a while, yeah?" The key to open communication is to find the right balance between directness, honesty, and tact.

When you adopt the 'never lie' mentality, you have to believe that everything will be better because of it. Everything *will* actually be better, but you have to believe it; otherwise, living it is difficult.

Over the years, I've learnt that the more open, honest, and transparent people are, the fewer friends they have. However, the relationships they do maintain are stronger than ever, especially when there's honesty on both sides.

So, what causes people to lie? For most of us – sociopaths excluded – it's an emotional response. If you look back at the lies you've told in the past, what fuelled those decisions? Often, emotions are the culprit.

The other thing to consider is when you start lying, where does it stop? One little lie to avoid an uncomfortable situation might seem okay. But what if that lie leads to another? What if you can't cover up the previous lies without telling a few more? Now you're up to your neck in bullshit, so you might as well tell another lie, right? Like anything, lies gain momentum. The more you tell, the more likely you are to pick up too much speed, lose control, and hit a wall of truth sooner or later.

History teaches us that dishonesty can have disastrous consequences for any company. Look at FTX, for example. Ultimately, the crypto exchange mishandled customer deposits and misled the public about what was actually happening behind the scenes. The company basically collapsed overnight. That's just one example of many where the lies and deceptive acts compounded to the point of ruin for the company involved. It's an extreme example, I know, but it illustrates the futility of taking a dishonest approach. FTX and others could have been successful without misleading anyone, but they chose the path of deception, and it backfired spectacularly.

Generally, if you look at transparency from a logical standpoint, honesty makes a lot more sense than the opposite. When you're always transparent, you don't have to keep looking over your shoulder. You know that a lie you told isn't going to come back and bite you on the arse one, two, or ten years down the track. As entrepreneurs, we're already stressed enough. Why add another worry to the pile?

DON'T PILLAGE THE COMMUNITY

In any ecosystem, community, whatever it may be, if you're only taking things out and not putting anything back in, you'll eventually drain it dry. It's energy exchange. Often, as a founder, people are giving you the energy you need to succeed. People's time, effort, and focus are going to you, which means they're not going to other people.

I know how valuable my time is and when I began getting opportunities to learn from some amazing people, I realised that others were likely missing out. Therefore, I felt a responsibility to give back to the community whenever I could. When I was in a position to help and educate others, I would do it. Like I said, my time is valuable and often quite limited, but other people had given me *their* valuable and limited time, so I owed it to the community to repay the debt. That's how you maintain a healthy ecosystem. You can't just take, take, take and expect your community to thrive. You have to give back, whether that's to peers, friends, family, wherever you've drawn energy and support from to reach your goals.

Once again, not having an agenda, aside from genuinely wanting to help, is important. If you really want to help and give back to the ecosystem, people will be receptive to that. Not only that, but they will absorb your give-back philosophy, and they will continue the practice when *they* reach success, creating an ecosystem that sustains itself.

THE FOUNDER-INVESTOR RELATIONSHIP

One of the toughest relationships to navigate can be the founder-investor relationship. I've been on both sides, so I understand where both parties are coming from. When someone invests in you and your idea, obviously there's money involved, which means the stakes can be quite high. As a founder, you don't want to waste an investor's money – in fact, you want to multiply it. As an investor, you want the same outcome. So, if everyone's goals are aligned, there shouldn't be any issues, right? That would be ideal, yeah.

The key to building a healthy founder-investor relationship is – you might have guessed it – trust. Without trust and transparency, you're in for a rough ride. Think about it. The typical founder-investor relationship lasts longer than the average marriage. I see a lot of startups that take the money because it's there, without considering the relationship they're entering into. If the two parties are incompatible or can't build that all-important trust, it causes issues for everyone later down the track. When the trust isn't there, an investor may decide to take a more hands-on approach to dictate the direction of the company and protect their investment, which, as founders, isn't what we generally want.

As an investor, I've learnt to have faith in the teams I've put my money behind. Really, I couldn't do it any other way. But the reason why I'm able to do that is because of the mutual trust between us. If things aren't tracking well, I trust that the team will turn it around. Of course, if everything were falling apart, I wouldn't be able to just sit back and let the business collapse. But entrepreneurs don't just need funding; they also need the time and space to make shit happen.

As a founder, you need to understand the tricky position investors are in. They've bet on you and your business, and naturally they want to win. They want *you* to succeed because it means they succeed. Transparency is critical in maintaining trust, and, to do what you do best, you need the complete backing of your supporters. You don't want to put any avoidable barriers in your way.

I would love to say that the power lies with the founder, but the reality is that the person handing out the money has the most leverage in the relationship. However, as a founder, you *do* have the power to choose who invests in your business. You don't have to take someone's money just because they've offered it. Depending on where your business is at, turning down capital can be super tough, especially if you need it to get to the next level. Sometimes, securing funding isn't just about getting a yes; it's about getting a yes from the right person. Most investors are cautious about who they get into bed with, and most founders should be too.

IT'S TIME TO EVALUATE YOUR RELATIONSHIPS

Often, you don't know that you've put effort into the wrong relationships until it's too late. Like everything that affects your business, you should analyse your relationships regularly. It may sound clinical, but it's necessary to ensure you're on the right track to reaching your goals. How can you know if you're investing in the wrong relationships if you aren't giving it much thought? On the flip side, how can you know that you're making good relationship investments if you aren't doing some sort of analysis? I know there's a huge emotional component to relationships that we can't overlook but by performing an analysis – no matter how clinical it may seem – you gain a better understanding of all the connections in your life and the parts they play. What you choose to do with that information is up to you.

Really, it's the new relationships that require the most scrutiny and, let's say, interrogation. *Does this relationship align with my objectives? Does it align with who I am and what I want to achieve? Does it fit my values? Is it worth the time and energy I'm putting into it?* If a relationship isn't propelling you towards your goals, that doesn't necessarily mean you need to cut that person off completely. It simply means the bulk of your energy would be best spent elsewhere.

At one time, I adopted the mindset that every relationship was an opportunity, even on a personal level. But when you go down that path, you get to a point where everything is being poorly executed. Whether I was getting involved with people or organisations, I was being pulled in too many different directions, and my focus was constantly being redirected. When you're working towards an objective, focus is crucial. You can't have people distracting you from your larger goals, which is why relationship analysis is so important. Which people in your life are your strongest assets? They're the relationships that are worthy of the biggest investment.

I'm not saying you should cut off everyone who's not adding awesome value to your life, but you don't want to string people along if you don't have energy to invest. The thing is, as long as you're honest and tactful, you can always pick those relationships up later if it makes sense to do so. I'm not in the business of burning bridges, but I also don't have the resources to maintain every bridge I encounter.

So, what does a valuable relationship look like? Let's use the example of a partner, whether that be girlfriend, boyfriend, husband, or wife. If you assess the typical romantic partnership, does it have value? Generally, yes. You have someone you can lean on and, in many cases, someone who has strengths that complement yours. If having children is one of your goals, a partner can help facilitate this. When you analyse the relationship, you can see that it has value.

Whether consciously or not, we frequently analyse our relationships in this way. Partners, friends, mentors – whatever the relationship, we're always looking for value add. It's natural. It's *human*. You might get along well with a lot of people, but not all of them are going to be your strongest assets. A conscious analysis helps you understand where your best assets are.

In business, we know we have to set clear objectives; otherwise, we get lost; we meander; we don't really get anywhere of note. It's the same in your personal life. When you know your destination, you can form and nurture the connections that make getting there easier. Essentially, it's all about creating the best conditions for success, both personally and professionally.

AVOID RELATIONSHIP OVERLOAD

Meaningful relationships are great, but the reality is you can only manage so many at any given time. Like I said, you get out what you put in, but your time and energy aren't infinite resources. You can only give so much, and you'll need to decide which relationships are worth the investment.

Sure, it would be great to have 100 BFFs who you can call at any time and receive an obligation-free favour, but then you've got 100 people who can call on *you* at any time for obligation-free favours and long D&Ms. And think of the social obligations — birthdays, weddings, dinner parties, this event, that event, simply meeting for coffee. If you try to maintain too many meaningful relationships, you'll spend most of your time supporting and socialising with your extensive friend list and little to no time working on your business, which isn't what we want.

Think of your capacity to give like a pie. You can divide it up into different-sized pieces, but you can't make more pie magically appear. Your partner will likely receive a big piece of the pie. Your best friend will also receive a good serving. Then you have to decide who else gets some pie and how much. Eventually, you'll be left with nothing but crumbs. If you want to give pie to someone else, you'll need to take it from someone who already has some. Hey, it's not a perfect analogy, but you get the point. You can't feed everyone in the village with one pie.

So, while meaningful connections should form naturally, you do have to decide which relationships to nurture. Like I said, trust is a big decider for me. If there's no trust, the relationship isn't worth maintaining. My time and energy would be better spent elsewhere. As you continue your entrepreneurial journey, you'll likely have to sacrifice some relationships along the way, which is fine. It's natural. As we move through life, our circles often change. You may have a couple of long-term friends who will always be there in some capacity, but many of the people who enter your life will leave. It's a fact of life. So, if someone isn't conducive to you achieving your goals or is actively holding you back from reaching the next stage, you may need to reconsider how much energy you're investing in the relationship. Would it be better spent elsewhere?

Essentially, relationships are the pillars of our lives. They hold up everything else. If you neglect the ones that matter, you threaten the structural integrity of your business and your life. If you focus on the wrong relationships, you risk instability and potentially total collapse. Our relationships matter. The key is determining which ones matter most.

KEY TAKEAWAYS FROM CHAPTER 11

1. Relationships have a compounding effect. Think wisely about how you interact with people and build meaningful relationships, because a lot of opportunities can come from playing the board game of relationships correctly.

2. Don't lie. Nothing good ever comes from it. Nothing. Ever.

3. Evaluate the time you are spending on your relationships and invest it wisely.

4. Relationships drive success. Cultivate relationships that are based on trust, mutual respect, and shared goals.

5. Create long-term partnerships. Focus on building long-term relationships that can grow and evolve with your business.

6. Boost emotional intelligence. Develop skills in empathy and communication to strengthen relationships.

7. Network diversely. Expand your network to include a wide variety of people from different backgrounds and industries.

THE FINE LINE BETWEEN MADNESS AND MASTERY

ow, what a journey we've taken together. From first grappling with the 'crazy or genius' question to learning the power of cultivating meaningful relationships, you're now intimately familiar with all the winning philosophies that took me – and will take you! – to the summit of success as an entrepreneur.

So, what separates the crazy from the genius in the world of entrepreneurship? It's all about perception and outcome. When an entrepreneur's ideas defy conventional wisdom and they challenge the status quo so fiercely that their vision borders on the absurd, they often earn the 'crazy' label. However, when an insane idea succeeds, society slaps the 'genius' label on them without a second thought. Evidently, the biggest defining factor is success. The hard part is earning that success, which is why I wrote this book.

As you know, the aim of *Crazy or Genius?* wasn't to provide a detailed blueprint of how to set up and scale a successful business. Instead, I chose to equip you with all the wisdom you need to navigate every step of your entrepreneurial journey with confidence. It's not just about *what* to do but also *how* you do it.

To be a successful entrepreneur, you must be bold enough to look beyond the horizon. You must have the courage to propose novel solutions to seemingly unsolvable problems. Let your passion, vision, and desire to bring your ideas to life drive you forward. You must not be afraid to charge into unchartered territory and take risks – calculated risks, that is – to create an impact in the world. When you push for true innovation, the line between insanity and brilliance can blur. That's where the magic happens.

As an entrepreneur, a visionary, a changemaker, you'll have some genius ideas. You'll have some crazy ones too. Let's be honest – some of your ideas will be downright silly. It's all a part of the entrepreneurial journey. You must be prepared to constantly navigate the line between risk and reward, madness and genius. The key is to not stray too far in the wrong direction.

My entrepreneurial journey and the philosophies I've forged along the way demonstrate that entrepreneurship isn't just about building businesses; it's also about challenging existing realities and being at the forefront of creating change. Each chapter, each philosophy, has prepared you to face the unpredictable, the difficult, and the seemingly insurmountable with wisdom and courage. Why repeat the mistakes of others when you can instead learn from them? Within the pages of *Crazy or Genius?*, I've given you the knowledge to smooth the road for the tough yet rewarding journey ahead. You now know exactly what you need to do to succeed as an entrepreneur. The next step? Get out there and do it.

What are you waiting for? The world is ready for your next genius idea, even if the majority label it crazy at first. If they do, you'll simply get the satisfaction of proving them wrong.

ACKNOWLEDGEMENTS

As I close the pages on this exploration of what it means to be an entrepreneur, I must pause and extend my deepest gratitude to those who have been the pillars through this entire journey: my family and my steadfast supporters.

To my family, thank you for your enduring patience and resilience, which have been my sanctuary and strength. You've witnessed my failures and my fleeting triumphs yet never wavered in your support. In the darkest times, when every day was a battle, your belief in me remained unshaken. You offered no judgements, only your unwavering support, asking for nothing in return.

I owe a special note of thanks to those who have shared in the burden of my dreams. You've been more than just friends or confidants; you've been partners in every sense, enduring long nights and endless challenges, always ready to lend a hand or an ear, without a trace of ego or expectation.

And to those who quietly cheered me on from the sidelines – your subtle nods of encouragement and simple acts of kindness have often been a beacon during my trying periods. Your belief in my potential has been as uplifting as any victory.

To all of you who have been part of this story, you have my enduring appreciation for keeping me grounded and for soaring with me when the winds were favourable. This book, and all it represents, is as much yours as it is mine. Here's to our continued journey, filled with learning, growth, and shared successes. Thank you for everything.

ABOUT THE AUTHOR

Martin Karafilis is an entrepreneur and author known for his innovative approach to business and his ability to turn complex challenges into opportunities for growth. With a career spanning various industries, Martin has consistently demonstrated his knack for identifying emerging trends and leading ventures from the ground up.

Martin's entrepreneurial journey began after a significant career shift, which propelled him into the world of startups and technology. His passion for innovation and commitment to excellence have resulted in multiple successful enterprises, each reflecting his vision for a future where technology enhances the quality of life.

As an author, Martin distils the lessons learnt from his experiences into actionable insights for aspiring entrepreneurs. This book is a testament to his belief in the power of resilience, strategic thinking, and personal growth.

Martin is also a dedicated advocate for continuous learning and believes in giving back to the community by mentoring young entrepreneurs and participating in various charitable activities. When he's not immersed in his business ventures, he enjoys spending time with his family and exploring the outdoors. **www.karafilis.me**

ENDNOTES

1   Chu, H 2020, *'Glitch' Died So Slack Could Take Over Offices Everywhere, but Traces of the Game Live On,* article, Mashable, viewed 10 December 2022, https://mashable.com/article/slack-glitch.

2   Collins, J 2011, *Good to Great: Why Some Companies Make the Leap… and Others Don't,* 1st edn, Harper Business.

3   Stoll, C 1995, *Why the Web Won't Be Nirvana,* online article, Newsweek, viewed 4 March 2023, https://www.newsweek.com/clifford-stoll-why-web-wont-be-nirvana-185306.

4   Summers, N 2010, *Let's Talk About the 1995 NEWSWEEK Piece That Says the Internet Will Fail,* online article, Newsweek, viewed 4 March 2023, https://www.newsweek.com/lets-talk-about-1995-newsweek-piece-says-internet-will-fail-210278.

5   Master of Business Administration n.d., *What Happened to Yahoo in 6 Points,* online article, University of Maryland, viewed 21 May 2023, https://onlinebusiness.umd.edu/blog/what-happened-to-yahoo-in-6-points/.

6   Mui, C 2021, *How Kodak Failed,* online article, Forbes, viewed 21 May 2023, https://www.forbes.com/sites/chunkamui/2012/01/18/how-kodak-failed/?sh=669608a56f27.

7   Satell, G 2014, *A Look Back at Why Blockbuster Really Failed and Why It Didn't Have to,* online article, Forbes, viewed 21 May 2023, https://www.forbes.com/sites/gregsatell/2014/09/05/a-look-back-at-why-blockbuster-really-failed-and-why-it-didnt-have-to/?sh=ccf5d031d64a.

AUDIOBOOK

Great news! *Crazy or Genius?* is also available in audio format.

In his audiobook, Martin includes bonus material and a few surprises to further help you on your entrepreneurial journey.

Jump onto your favourite audiobook platform now and check it out.

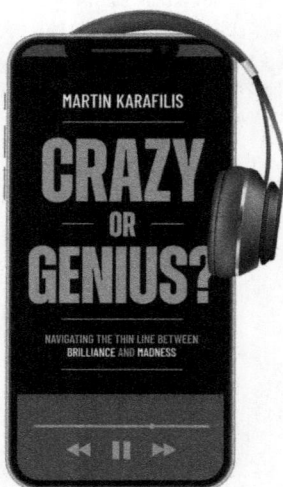

audible an amazon company 🍎 **Spotify**